LANDLORD OR TENANT?

A View of Irish History

BOOKS BY THE SAME AUTHOR

BC: The Archaeology of the Bible Lands
Introducing Archaeology
Viking Expansion Westwards
Hammer of the North
The Clacken and the Slate

TRANSLATIONS OF
ICELANDIC SAGAS

The Vinland Sagas
Njal's Saga
Laxdæla Saga
King Harald's Saga

TRANSLATIONS OF NOVELS BY
HALLDOR LAXNESS

The Atom Station
Paradise Reclaimed
The Fish Can Sing
World Light
Christianity Under Glacier

LANDLORD OR TENANT?

A View of Irish History

Magnus Magnusson

Research by HELEN FRY

THE BODLEY HEAD
LONDON   SYDNEY
TORONTO

Published by arrangement with the
British Broadcasting Corporation

British Library Cataloguing
in Publication Data
Magnusson, Magnus
Landlord or tenant?
1. Ireland – History – 1172
I. Title
941.5   DA 933
ISBN 0-370-30130-7

© 1978 Magnus Magnusson
Printed in Great Britain for
The Bodley Head Ltd
9 Bow Street, London WC2E 7AL
by Redwood Burn Ltd, Trowbridge
set in Photon Plantin
First published 1978

CONTENTS

FOREWORD

This little book is an expanded version of a four-part series of radio programmes that I wrote and presented for BBC Radio 4 in September 1977 (repeated in October 1978) under the title *Landlord or Tenant?* It aroused considerable interest in Britain, and also overseas after an abbreviated version was broadcast on the BBC World Service; and I welcome this opportunity to publish it in book form, especially since it allows me to include contemporary source material which I had previously had to discard to fit the Procrustean bed of a 45-minute time slot.

My major debt is to my producer, Helen Fry, who is Chief Producer, Archive Features (Radio) at the BBC. It was her original idea; she commissioned and researched the series, and my journeyings round Ireland were constantly enlivened by her stimulating company and wide background knowledge of the subject. To cap it all, she has sought and supplied all the illustrations that appear in this book. I cannot thank her enough.

This is essentially a layman's book. I went to Ireland in all humility to try to find out for myself the historical background to the present tensions there. I am deeply grateful to the many scholars on both sides of the Border who gave freely of their time while I relentlessly picked their brains: Professor R. Dudley Edwards (University College, Dublin), Professor E. R. R. Green (Queen's University, Belfast), Professor David W. Harkness (Queen's University, Belfast), Professor F. S. L. Lyons (Provost of Trinity College, Dublin), Dr M. McCurtain [Sister Benvenuta] (University College, Dublin), Professor Theodore Moody (Trinity College, Dublin, now retired), Professor J. A. Murphy (University College, Cork), Dr Conor Cruise O'Brien (now Editor-in-Chief of the *Observer*), Liam de Paor (University College, Dublin), and Dr Maire de Paor (University College, Cork), and Dr J. H. Whyte (Queen's University, Belfast). I

7

am also indebted to the Director and staff of the Public Record Office of Northern Ireland.

It is to them, above all, that this book is dedicated, and to all those others who are working patiently and unspectacularly in classrooms and lecture rooms to instil in future generations a greater understanding of the realities of Irish history.

Any errors of fact or judgement that may occur in these pages are, of course, my own fault and not their responsibility; but if there are only a few, this is largely due to the contribution of two valued friends and colleagues: Douglas Carson, who is Senior Schools Producer (Radio) in BBC Northern Ireland, and Owen Dudley Edwards, of Edinburgh University, scion of a redoubtable dynasty of Irish historians. They went through the original radio scripts and this book with painstaking care and concern, correcting misapprehensions and adding many felicitous suggestions of their own.

MAGNUS MAGNUSSON

PART I

Given to
Foreign Tribes:
1541-1690

Just about the first thing I saw as I drove into Dublin from the airport was an advertising hoarding. The product was so familiar, so much part of the Irish scene, that it needed no brand name to identify it: just a small golden harp superimposed on a glass of dark and creamy stout. The slogan was discreet, but unmistakable. It said, simply, 'Take up Irish History tonight'.

It seemed to me then a remarkably apposite invitation; for that was precisely what I had had in mind in going to Ireland—to take up Irish history. Not, I hasten to say, as an historian, for that I am not; but as a journalist. As an enquirer. As an *ignorant* enquirer, I should confess at the outset.

I do not think I am exceptional in that respect. In the past, Irish history has all too often been seen as through a glass, darkly. Or if you were brought up and educated in Scotland or England, as I was, it wasn't seen at all—except, perhaps, as a footnote to Britain's imperial history.

My own schooling had left me dimly aware of a series of sombre and highly charged occasions: the Norman invasion of Ireland in the twelfth century; the Tudor reconquest in the sixteenth century; the so-called 'Plantation' of Protestant settlers in Ulster early in the seventeenth century; the alleged massacre of Protestants in 1641; the invasion by Cromwell; the Battle of the Boyne in 1690, when, in the crude words of the song, 'King Billy slew the Papish crew, at the Battle of Boyne Water'. And so it went on, this sad and

9

passionate litany of wars and rebellions and causes to die for; the pride and the pain, the myths and the martyrs, all inextricably intertwined.

The imposition of the Penal Laws against Catholics; Grattan's Parliament, and the abortive rising of 1798; the glowing promise and ultimate frustration of Daniel O'Connell; the appalling years of the Potato Famine in the 1840s, when a million died and a million emigrated, and the British government was accused of downright, uncompromising genocide; the Fenians, and the Home Rule movement under Parnell; the Easter Rising of 1916, the Troubles, and the Partition of Ireland in 1921.

And today, as a direct legacy of this ferocious history, the present troubles in Northern Ireland: a civil war held in check only by the presence of a referee whom the extremists on both sides want to see out of the ring, so that they can fight dirty—even dirtier than before.

It seemed to me that it was more than high time to try to clarify for myself the perspectives of Irish history. I happen to believe that there is an absolute value in the study of history, in the contemplation of man in society in the past, in order to achieve a greater understanding of the present—and, ideally, to temper the future. 'What's past is prologue,' wrote Shakespeare in *The Tempest*. In Ireland, the study of history has an even keener relevance than elsewhere, because the Irish are nurtured on the past and tend not to forget or forgive the 'wrongs' of that past.

Sometimes, it can be argued, these 'wrongs' can be shown to have been wrongly interpreted, whether deliberately or not. History has been used in Ireland as *story*, as a rich and passionate source of rhetoric for the next plunge into bitter violence. Perhaps if we all had a greater understanding of how things happened, and why things happened, we might have more sympathy for one another's standpoints. In the wise words of Professor F. S. L. Lyons, Provost of Trinity College, Dublin: 'To understand the past fully is to cease to live in it, and to cease to live in it is to take the earliest steps towards shaping what is to come from the material of the present.'

It may seem a little naive to believe that a more rational and compassionate understanding of the past can solve many present predicaments. I don't suppose that a gunman planning to shoot you would be deflected from his intent if you pointed out to him that most Irish historians, both Catholic and Protestant, no longer believe that the catastrophe of the Potato Famine was due to some devious British policy of genocide— rather, it was the outcome of economic forces which neither the British, nor anyone else in the context of the time, were capable of dealing with. It might seem too academic an argument for the occasion.

But that's a somewhat crude way of putting it. Understanding—on all sides—is a long-term process. The fact is, as I discovered when I went to seek enlightenment from Irish historians both north and south of the Border, the past forty years have seen another kind of revolution taking place in Ireland: what is now being called the Historiographical Revolution—a substantial re-writing, or revision, of Irish history, based on professional academic disciplines rather than on traditional myths and prejudices.

And from this latest and least violent of Irish revolutions, some surprising things have emerged. For instance, from a people brought up to believe that most of its ills could be traced to predatory alien landlords oppressing the wretched native peasants, has come a scholarly study entitled *Predatory Peasants and Downtrodden Landlords!* To a northern enclave obsessed with the Protestant victory at the Battle of the Boyne has come the appalled recognition that King William, the Orangeman's hero, invaded Catholic Ireland with the blessing of the Pope himself! It is this sort of modification of traditional and fiercely held views that I am seeking to report in this short account.

The Tudor Conquest

'He that would England win,
Let him in Ireland first begin.'

But where in Irish history do *we* begin? Do we start with the
first recorded traces of Stone Age man in prehistoric times,
around 7000 BC—hunting groups who seem to have migrated
from Scandinavia via Britain? Do we start with the influx of
the first Stone Age farmers around 4000 BC—the first people
to clear forest-land and plant grain in those newly created
fields? The people, perhaps from Brittany, who were to build
the great prehistoric grave-monuments at Knowth and New-
grange?

Do we start at the onset of the Christian era, when a new
race, the Celts from central Europe, had established themselves in Ireland with their formidable iron weapons? To the
Roman armies which then occupied England, Ireland seemed
altogether too forbidding a prospect, and they left it strictly
alone.

Do we start with the fifth century AD, when Ireland emerges
into history proper as a pastoral country divided into several
petty kingdoms, on the threshold of a golden age of Celtic
Christianity, when monasteries dominated the land and Irish
missionaries spread their learning and their message throughout Europe? Or do we start with the time of the Viking incur-
sions in the ninth century, when these intrepid sea-rovers and
merchants brought Ireland into the mainstream of European
commerce for the first time by founding trading cities like
Dublin and Waterford and Wexford?

Do we start with the Anglo-Norman invasion of Ireland,
which did not begin until a full century after the 1066 Conquest of England? That was the time when adventurous
Welsh-Norman warrior knights like Richard Fitzgilbert de
Clare, Earl of Pembroke, better known by the resounding
nickname of 'Strongbow', began to infiltrate Irish society by
force of arms and studded the land with some three thousand

stout Norman castles and tower houses. It would certainly seem logical, because the Anglo-Norman invasion in the twelfth century is said to have changed the destinies of Ireland more than any other event in history, apart from the arrival of St Patrick and his fellow missionaries.

But the Norman Conquest of Ireland was only half a conquest. Norman barons controlled much of the country, they developed new patterns of trade—but they never succeeded in doing what they had done in England: creating a new nation that combined the characteristics of natives and incomers alike. By the fourteenth century, indeed, Ireland was still a deeply divided country.

So perhaps we should start with the year 1541, when King Henry VIII, one of the most celebrated monarchs in English history, made himself King of Ireland as well, and brought Ireland formally into the embryonic British empire. In that year, the Irish Parliament, an assembly of magnates which had been evolving under English domination, passed *An Act that the King of England, his Heirs and Successors, be Kings of Ireland*:

'Forasmuch as . . . the Irish men and inhabitants within this Realm of Ireland have not been so obedient to the King's Highness and his most noble progenitors, and to their laws, as they of right and according to their allegiance and bounden duties ought to have been: wherefore at the humble pursuit, petition, and request of the lords spiritual and temporal, and other the King's loving, faithful, and obedient subjects of this his land of Ireland, and by their full assents, be it enacted, ordained and established by authority of this present Parliament, that the King's Highness, his heirs and successors, Kings of England, be always Kings of this land of Ireland . . . to have, hold, and enjoy the said style, title, majesty, and honours of King of Ireland . . . as united and knit to the imperial crown of the Realm of England.'

13

Many historians see this as the crucial date in Ireland's history, the start of the modern period and the beginning of the emergence of the State, as such. Before then, kings of England had claimed the title of Lord of Ireland, but their writ did not run far. In most parts of Ireland the crown had little or no power or presence at all; only in Dublin and the surrounding areas did the King's representatives have much sway—an uneasy royal enclave formalised by the construction of the Pale. The Pale was a physical structure, a stockade protected by a ditch, which by Henry's time enclosed the four counties of Louth, Meath, Dublin and Kildare. The word 'Pale' simply means 'fence', and it was from this that the English language derived that arrogantly condescending phrase, 'beyond the Pale', meaning 'beyond the bounds of civilised behaviour'.

Henry achieved his aim with his familiar political techniques of bullying and bribing. The bullying came first, in the form of a series of punitive expeditions against the Irish lords throughout the country, to force them to submit to Henry's authority. The most spectacular and violent of these was the ruthless suppression in 1535 of a rebellion by Thomas Fitzgerald, son of the Earl of Kildare. The Fitzgerald stronghold of Maynooth Castle was pounded to submission by artillery fire, and the survivors who surrendered were given what came to be known ironically as 'the pardon of Maynooth': they were put to death.

Then came the bribing: the King persuaded the native Irish lords to support him by *giving* them their lands (and titles to go with them), even though these lands were clan lands and traditionally held by the chieftains only on behalf of the clans; clan fealty would now be legally replaced by crown feudalism.

This was the background to the apparent Irish enthusiasm for the Act that Sir Anthony St Leger, Lord Deputy to the King, duly reported to His Majesty in a letter from Dublin dated 26 June 1541:

'. . . it was by me, your poor servant, proposed, that forasmuch as your Majesty had always been the only protector and defender, under God, of this Realm, that it was most meet that your Majesty, and your heirs, should from thenceforth be named and called KING of the same; and caused the Bill devised for the same to be read; which once being read, and declared to them, in Irish, all the whole House most willingly and joyously consented and agreed to the same. And being three times read, and with one voice agreed, we sent the same to the Lower House, where, in like wise it passed, with no less joy and willing consent.'

Tudor policy towards Ireland was one of aggressive anglicisation. There were some sixty native Irish lords or chieftains 'beyond the Pale' at the time, traditional dynasts who ruled their territories independently of England. There were also the Old English, as they were called, Anglo-Norman lords who had adopted Irish ways and were doubtful in their allegiance to the crown. By the time of Henry's death in 1547, forty powerful chieftains had submitted to the crown. Henry's policy towards all those 'beyond the Pale' was to try to destroy the essential distinctiveness of Irish society—their language, their laws, and their social traditions—and to create out of the divided country one nation, one kind of people: anglicised subjects of the King. There were no half measures about Henry VIII's *Act for the English Order, Habit and Language*:

'Wherefore be it enacted . . . that no person or persons, the King's subjects within this land being . . . shall be shorn, or shaven above the ears, or use the wearing of hair upon their heads, like unto long locks called "glibes" or have or use any hair growing upon their upper lips, called or named a "crommeal", or use or wear any shirt, smock, kerchief . . . or linen cap, coloured or dyed with saffron, nor yet use, or wear in any their shirts or smocks above 7 yards of cloth, to be measured according to the King's standard,

15

and that also no woman use or wear any "kyrtell" [skirt], or coat tucked up, or embroidered or garnished with silk, nor couched nor laid with "usker" [ornaments] after the Irish fashion; and that no person or persons . . . shall use or wear any mantles, coat or hood made after the Irish fashion . . .

'And be it enacted that every person or persons, the King's true subjects, inhabiting this land of Ireland, of what estate, condition or degree he or they be, or shall be, to the uttermost of their power, cunning and knowledge, shall use and speak commonly the English tongue and language . . . [and] shall bring up . . . his . . . children in such places, where they shall or may have occasion to learn the English tongue, order and condition.'

Henry's motives for initiating what is known as the Tudor Reconquest of Ireland were doubtless complex. One of them must surely have derived from the example of his father, Henry VII, the founder of the Tudor dynasty. Henry VII had shown that there were more ways of invading England than by the front door, across the Channel; he had come in by the back door, through Wales. Ireland represented even more of a back door, and a highly vulnerable one at that. 'He that would England win, Let him in Ireland first begin,' as the old ditty had it. Ireland was dangerous to the English crown as a potential base for either domestic rivals or foreign enemies.

The Tudors had a shrewd instinct for survival; and over Ireland they showed themselves to be prescient. Ireland was moving on to the stage of international politics, and first Spain, and more particularly France, would make frequent attempts to use Ireland in their wars with England. English concern about their vulnerable flank to the west was never completely allayed, and goes a long way towards explaining, if not justifying, much of the severity of England's policy towards Ireland down the centuries.

Henry VIII also had a politico-religious motive. For reasons of power rather than of piety, he had exploited the Reformation movement while not embracing its principles. In order to extend his supremacy over the Church to Ireland, he had to change Ireland's constitution; his title of Lord of Ireland had been granted by the Pope, so that if he was going to undertake the dissolution of the monasteries in Ireland, he had to repudiate papal authority and assume the kingship of Ireland, as he had assumed the headship of the Church of England.

But the Reformation had little impact on Ireland, at the time anyway, except in the towns and within the Pale, where most of the religious houses were promptly dissolved. There was no popular support for it, no widespread resentment against the Papacy or the Catholic Church. Even when Edward VI succeeded Henry, there was no mass acceptance of Protestantism in Ireland. The old ways continued; and when Mary Tudor, who would restore the old religion, came to the throne in 1553, there was general rejoicing, much to the chagrin of a convinced Protestant convert like John Bale, the extreme and unpopular English Bishop of Ossory. He had been nominated to the see of Ossory by Edward VI in 1552; in the following year he described how the people of Kilkenny, anticipating Mary Tudor's restoration of Catholicism, rejoiced at her accession. John Bale left Ireland shortly afterwards and went to Switzerland where he wrote *The Vocation of John Bale to the Bishopric of Ossory in Ireland, his Persecutions in the same, and Final Deliverance*:

'On the twentieth day of August, was the Lady Mary with us at Kilkenny proclaimed Queen of England, France and Ireland, with the greatest solemnity that there could be devised, of processions, musters and disguisings; all the noble captains and gentlemen thereabout being present. What-a-do I had that day with the prebendaries and priests about wearing the cope, crosier and mitre in procession, it were too much to write . . . On the Thursday, which was the last day of August, I being absent, the clergy of Kilkenny, by procurement of that wicked justice Hothe, blasphemously resumed again the whole Papism, or heap of superstitions of the Bishop of Rome; to the utter contempt of Christ and His holy Word, of the King and Council of England, and of all ecclesiastical and politic order, without either statute or yet proclamation. They rung all the bells in that cathedral, minster, and parish churches: they flung up their caps to the battlement of the great temple, with smilings and laughings most dissolutely . . . they brought forth their copes, candle sticks, holy-water stock, cross and censers; they mustered forth in general procession most gorgeously, all the town over, with *Sancta Maria, ora pro nobis,* and the rest of the Latin litany: they chattered it, they chanted it, with great noise and devotion: they banqueted all the day after, for that they were delivered from the grace of God into a warm sun.'

The rejoicing at Kilkenny was short-lived, however. Queen Elizabeth's accession only five years later, in 1558, led to a reversion to the policy of trying to impose Protestantism on Ireland. But opposition to change now grew much stiffer, led by the missionary orders of the Continental Counter-Reformation, and supported by the Old English and Gaelic Irish alike, who saw the established Anglican Church of Ireland as representative of an alien government. The Irish Parliament, too, represented only the more anglicised areas of the country. Ireland, in effect, was governed by a succession of skilled and subtle civil servants from the court of Elizabeth; and where persuasion did not work, they wasted little time before using force. An English standing army became a permanent feature of Irish life.

The 'pacification' of Ireland, as the English Elizabethan would have called it, proceeded apace as the sixteenth century went on. At the time of England's most dangerous hour—the attempted invasion by the Spanish Armada in 1588—there were relatively few Irishmen who were prepared to give any aid whatsoever to the wretched survivors of those Spanish ships that were wrecked on Ireland's cruel coasts: quite the opposite in some cases, where the records suggest that the natives were not averse to helping the survivors into the next life. It provoked one Spanish captain, Don Francisco de Cuellar, a typical man of the Renaissance, to take a somewhat jaundiced view of the social *mores* of the Irish.

'The custom of these savages is to live as the brute beasts among the mountains, which are very rugged in that part of Ireland where we lost ourselves. They live in huts made of straw. The men are all large-bodied, and of handsome features and limbs; and as active as the roe deer. They do not eat oftener than once a day, and this is at night; and that which they usually eat is butter with oaten bread . . .

'On feast days they eat some flesh half-cooked, without bread or salt, as that is their custom. They clothe themselves, according to their habit, with tight trousers, and short loose coats of very coarse goat's hair. They cover themselves with "mantas" [blankets] and wear their hair down to their eyes. They are great walkers, and inured to toil. They carry on perpetual war with the English, who here keep garrison for the Queen, from whom they defend themselves, and do not let them enter their territory, which is subject to inundation and marshy . . .

'The chief inclination of these people, is to be robbers, and to plunder each other; so that no day passes without a call to arms among them. For the people in one village becoming aware that in another there are cattle or other effects, they immediately come armed in the night . . . and kill one another; and the English from the garrisons, getting to know who had taken and robbed most cattle, then come down upon them, and carry away the plunder. They have therefore, no other remedy but to withdraw themselves to the mountains, with their women and cattle; for they possess no other property nor more movables nor clothing. They sleep upon the ground, on rushes, newly cut and full of water and ice.

'The most of the women are very beautiful, but badly dressed. They do not wear more than a chemise, and a blanket, with which they cover themselves, and a linen cloth, much doubled, over the head, and tied in front. They are great workers and housekeepers, after their fashion. These people call themselves Christians. Mass is said among them, and regulated according to the orders of the Church of Rome. The great majority of their churches, monasteries, and hermitages, have been demolished by the hands of the English, who are in garrison . . .

'In short in this Kingdom there is neither justice or right, and everyone does what he pleases.'

Others took a much more lyrical view of Elizabethan Ireland—courtiers like the poet Edmund Spenser, author of *The Faerie Queen*, that elegantly allegorical eulogy of Queen Elizabeth. He was appointed secretary to Lord Grey de Wilton, Lord Deputy in Ireland, and was given a castle and some land there for his services. An extract from his essay on Ireland gives the flavour of his attitude:

'And sure it is yet a most beautiful and sweet country as any is under Heaven, seamed throughout with many goodly rivers, replenished with all sorts of fish, most abundantly sprinkled with many sweet islands and goodly lakes, like little inland seas, that will carry even ships upon their waters, adorned with goodly woods fit for building of houses and ships, so commodiously, that if some princes in the world had them, they would soon hope to be lords of all the seas, and ere long of all the world; also full of good ports and havens opening upon England and Scotland, as inviting us to come to them, to see what excellent commodities that country can afford, besides the soil itself most fertile, fit to yield all kind of fruit that shall be committed thereunto. And lastly, the heavens most mild and temperate, though somewhat more moist in the part toward the West.'

Beneath that serene, idealised picture, some modern historians have detected a subtle sales pitch for the imperial exploitation of England's first colony—useful harbours and havens, timber for building a navy. Indeed, many of the Tudor imperial entrepreneurs like Walter Raleigh and Humphrey Gilbert 'practised' in Ireland before trying their hand across the Atlantic. But in Ireland, Queen Elizabeth's efforts to unify the Irish nation under Protestantism were getting nowhere. Although there were statutes under which Catholics could be severely prosecuted, Elizabeth seems to have been markedly tolerant about enforcing them. The masses of the people clung stubbornly to their old religion, as the Anglican Bishop of Cork and Ross complained in a letter to Lord Hunsdon in 1596:

'Our state here is very dangerous . . . Here are five justices of peace that sit on the bench every sessions, but they never took the Oath of Supremacy to Her Majesty, nor will. Two of them utterly refused at the general sessions holden in March last. Hereby they are generally mightily drawn away from their loyalty to Her Majesty's godly laws now within these two years so far, that where I had a thousand or more in a church at sermon, I now have not five; and whereas I have seen 500 communicants or more, now are there not three . . . I have caused churches to be re-edified, and provided books for every church through my diocese, as Bibles, New Testaments, Communion Books, both English and Latin . . . but none will come to the church at all, not so much as the country churls; they follow their seducers the priests and their superiors.'

One area in particular had steadily resisted Elizabeth's policy of anglicisation, and that was Ulster. The former kingdom of Ulster had remained a rather separate enclave, islanded by the geographical features that served so well to defend it—the sea, the lakes, the surrounding mountains and forests. The lords of Ulster had always nursed a profound suspicion of English political intentions, and some would say with good reason, for the Queen's agents were believed to have been behind innumerable acts of violence in Ulster.

In the 1590s, the long and bitter resentments flared into a major rebellion against the crown; and for the last nine years of her reign Elizabeth was embroiled in a war that historians now recognise as having placed an almost intolerable strain on England's stretched resources. The Nine Years' War, it is now called: the last major conflict of the Tudor dynasty. Ulster was the only remaining bastion of the old Ireland and her Gaelic institutions, and the outcome of this clash would decide the destiny of Ireland as a nation for generations.

The leader of the Ulster rebels was the charismatic Earl of Tyrone, Hugh O'Neill, descendant of kings. He proved himself a magnificent guerrilla leader, harrying and harassing, ambushing English columns, seldom giving battle except on his own terms. Elizabeth sent her favourite, the Earl of Essex, to lead the royal forces, and he has left us an account of the difficulties of campaigning against the rebels.

'This war is like to exercise both our faculties that do manage it, and Her Majesty's patience that must maintain it; for this people against whom we fight hath able bodies, a good use of the arms they carry, boldness enough to attempt, and quickness in apprehending any advantage they see offered them; whereas our new and common sort of men have neither bodies, spirits, nor practice of arms like the others. The advantage we have is more horse, which will command all champaigns [level and open country]; in our order, which these savages have not; and in the extraordinary courage and spirit of our men of quality. But, to meet with these our helps, the rebels fight in woods and bogs, where horse are utterly unserviceable; they use the advantage of lightness and swiftness in going off, when they find our order too strong for them to encounter: and as for the last advantage, I protest to your Lordships it doth as much trouble me as help me, for my remembering how unequal a wager it is to adventure the lives of noblemen and gentlemen against rogues and naked beggars, makes me take more care to contain our best men, than to use their courages against the rebels . . .'

However, O'Neill knew well that Ulster alone could not drive the English out of Ireland, and he constantly sought to spread the war to involve the whole country. But he also looked farther afield for help—to England's arch-enemy, Spain. On 5 October 1595 he sent an appeal to King Philip II through a Spanish nobleman, Don Carillo:

'The faith might be re-established in Ireland within one year, if the King of Spain would send only 3,000 soldiers. All the heretics would disappear, and no other sovereign would be recognised than the King Catholic. Both I and O'Donnell have besought him to succour the Church. Pray second our petition. If we obtain positive assurance of succour from the King, we will make no peace with the heretics.'

On 22 June 1596 the King of Spain replied in a letter to O'Neill:

'I have been informed you are defending the Catholic cause against the English. That this is acceptable to God is proved by the signal victories which you have gained. I hope you will continue to prosper: and you need not doubt but I will render you any assistance you may require. Give credence to Fussius, the bearer, and acquaint him with your affairs and your wishes.'

The Spanish Council of State provided for the King persuasive political arguments in favour of taking Ireland:

'Your Majesty would gain enormously in prestige by

23

conquering a kingdom thus unexpectedly.

'The bridle which the possession of Ireland by your Majesty would put upon England and the northern powers, would enable you to divert them from all other points of attack, and prevent them from molesting Spain, the Indies, etc. It would also enable you to make good terms of peace and recover the Flemish fortresses held by the English for the rebels.

'In the case of the Queen's death, your Majesty, as master of Ireland, would be in a greatly improved position to nominate a successor to the English crown.'

To the English, of course, O'Neill's appeal to Spain was the ultimate treachery, and may well be the basis of the hatred, fuelled by fear, which the English upper classes were to display towards the Irish from then on. Certainly, it was the ultimate vindication of the Tudor policy of trying to block the back door into England. Tudor fears were being fulfilled: European enemies were using Ireland to endanger the realm of England. In 1598, the Lords Justices and the rest of the Council in Ireland wrote to the Privy Council in London:

'We have daily advertisements of Tyrone's treacherous practices to extend his rebellion and treason into all parts of the Realm, having his ministers to pass to and fro through every province and other country of the Kingdom, labouring to seduce the people, by many colourable offers and pretences, to right them in their supposed Irish claims and titles to land and countries, long since lawfully evicted from them, and to introduce Papistry, which he beginneth now to make a more firm ground of his rebellion than he did before, insinuating that he is borne up and maintained therein by the Spanish King, by which course he hath wrought dangerous impressions in the hearts of the people . . . yet we are of opinion that it is not religion, nor old beggarly titles, that do carry him, but that it is the alteration

of the Government and State that he aimeth at, as by his
letters, which we have formerly signified to your Lordships, he hath promised to the Spaniards, and is still coun-
tenanced and encouraged therein by them.'

Help from Spain was not immediately forthcoming, however. In April 1600, nearly five years after O'Neill's first
appeal for help from Spain, a Spanish prelate in Ireland,
Matthew de Oviedo, sent a situation report to Philip of Spain:

'I came to Ireland by your Majesty's orders to obtain full
information from the Catholics, and urge them to continued zeal in the service of the faith of your Majesty . . . I
can assert that your Majesty has in this island the most
brave and faithful vassals that any king can have, such,
indeed, that if they were not already devoted to Spain, it
would be necessary to obtain their adhesion by all possible
means.

'As the oft-promised aid from Spain was hourly expected,
when we arrived with empty hands, only again to repeat the
old promises, they were overcome with sorrow and dismay,
especially as they had news of the enemy in force, both by
land and sea. Although O'Neill and O'Donnell are full of
courage, they cannot prevail over the other chiefs their followers, who fear the long delay in the arrival of succour,
and suspect that they are being played with. We have done
our best to stiffen them by every possible argument, assur-
ing them of your Majesty's desire to help them . . . and
promising that succour shall be sent by your Majesty with
all speed. This has tranquillised them somewhat, and they
promise to wait five months, as they think that they cannot
in any case hold out longer than that without help . . . They
have done great things this summer, and O'Neill has overrun all Munster and submitted it to your Majesty, whilst
O'Donnell has subjected Connacht. That your Majesty
may understand what you possess in these Catholics, I may
say that O'Neill had almost prevailed upon the Earl of

Essex to desert the Queen's cause and join that of your Majesty, and surrender all the Realm to you. O'Neill in the course of the negotiations promised him, Essex, on behalf of your Majesty, that you would show him signal favour, and as Essex was distrustful in consequence of certain injuries he had inflicted on Spain, O'Neill gave him his son as a hostage. What more could the most loyal Spaniard have done? . . . I remain here according to orders, anxiously hoping to do good service to the Church and your Majesty.'

There is no way now of telling whether this allegation of perfidy by Essex was fact or propaganda fiction, but it served its purpose. Eventually the Spaniards did come, in the late summer of 1601. They landed at Kinsale, near Cork, where they were promptly besieged. O'Neill marched his troops to meet them. Ironically, it was the arrival of the Spaniards that proved O'Neill's undoing, for now he was forced to do what he had always astutely avoided: he went on the offensive, and took on the English forces in a set-piece battle on their terms. Here, the Irish levies proved no match for the well-trained English army, and they were routed. The Spaniards were then winkled out of the town of Kinsale without much difficulty, and soon Ulster itself was overrun; then in 1603 Hugh O'Neill himself formally submitted. He had been holding out desperately in the hope that Queen Elizabeth would die and that he might achieve better terms from her successor. Ironically, he did not know that she had in fact died a week before his submission.

The Nine Years' War had given Elizabethan England a shock. It had also cost the Exchequer two million pounds sterling. It had ended in a negotiated settlement which allowed the Ulster leaders to return to their lands—not as independent lords but as landlords subject to the English crown. There is some suspicion that O'Neill may have got himself involved in a plot against Elizabeth's successor, James I, but whatever the reason, after four years of chafing under the

English supremacy, O'Neill and ninety of the leading men of Ulster went into voluntary exile on the Continent. This 'Flight of the Earls', as it has been called, left Ulster, the last Gaelic bastion, leaderless, and left English authority in control of every part of Ireland for the first time. It also opened the way to one of the most fateful and emotive events in Ireland's history: the Ulster Plantation.

The Ulster Plantation

'Plantation', or planned resettlement by colonists loyal to the crown, was not a new idea. The Tudors had tried it in a small way in central Ireland, but English yeomen farmers had been reluctant to leave their own broad acres for pioneering unbroken land in Ireland, and little had come of these early attempts to 'plant' English immigrants and thus create a stable Protestant landowning class to keep the Irish Catholics in check.

The Ulster Plantation was planned on a much larger scale. By confiscating huge tracts of land and expelling the natives, the population balance in the counties of Armagh, Cavan, Donegal, Derry, Fermanagh and Tyrone was to be drastically changed—the 'final solution', as it were, to the problem of the troublesome Gaelic enclave in the north. From 1609 onwards new settlers arrived in droves, year after year. Unlike the earlier experiments, this massive human transplant took. Many of the settlers came from Lowland Scotland; and they were not only landed gentry, they came from all classes. They cleared the land of forests, they ploughed their fields, they built their own towns and villages. For the Lowland Scots Ulster was a natural extension, almost a natural overspill area. A contemporary report on Sir Hugh Montgomery's plantation in County Down gives a vivid picture of how the newcomers settled in:

'They soon made cottages and booths for themselves, because sods and saplings of ashes, alders, and birch trees
(above thirty years old) with rushes for thatch, and bushes
for wattles, were at hand. And also they made a shelter of
the said stump of the castle for Sir Hugh, whose residence
was mostly there, as in the centre of being supplied with
necessaries from Belfast (but six miles thence), who therefore came and set up a market in Newtown, for profit for
both the towns. As likewise in the fair summer season
(twice, sometimes thrice every week) they were supplied
from Scotland, as Donaghadee was oftener, because but
three hours' sail from Port Patrick, where they bespoke
provisions and necessaries to lade in, to be brought over by
their own or that town's boats whenever wind and weather
served them, for there was a constant flux of passengers
coming daily over.

'I have heard honest old men say that in June, July, and
August, 1607, people came from Stranraer, four miles, and
left their horses at the port, hired horses at Donaghadee,
came with their wares and provisions to Newtown, and sold
them, dined there, stayed two or three hours, and returned
to their houses the same day by bed-time, their land journey
but twenty miles . . . Such was their encouragement from a
ready market, and their kind desires to see and supply their
friends and kindred, which commerce took quite away the
evil report of wolves and wood-kerne, which enviers of
planter's industry had raised and brought upon our planta-
tions . . .'

These alien Scottish settlers brought with them their own
customs and institutions. Of particular importance for the
future history of Ireland was that they eventually established
a Presbyterian Church, and thus a third tribal strand was
injected into this divided country: the episcopalian landed
gentry and middle class of the established Church of Ireland,

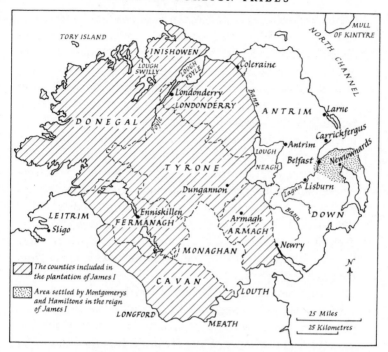

the Presbyterian Protestants, and the Catholic Irish. In time it would lead to a virulent form of religious apartheid, in which members of the Church of Ireland were, metaphorically, the privileged ruling whites, the Presbyterians were the Cape Coloureds, and the Catholics were the blacks.

Any hopes the Irish Catholics might have entertained that King James I would permit or even tolerate some easing of the sanctions against their religion were quickly dashed. On 4 July 1605, the King issued a *Proclamation against Toleration in Ireland*:

'[James I] is informed that his subjects in the Realm of Ireland have since the decease of Queen Elizabeth, been much abused by an untrue suggestion and report to the effect that he purposes to give liberty of conscience or toleration of religion to his subjects in that Kingdom, contrary to the express laws and statutes therein enacted, and to that uniformity of religion which has ever been constantly professed by him and is universally used and observed in his other dominions and countries. This false rumour is not only a secret imputation upon him, as if he were more remiss or less careful in the government of the Church of Ireland than of those other Churches whereof he has the supreme charge, but also divers of his subjects in that Kingdom are heartened and encouraged to continue in their superstition and recusancy; and such Jesuits, seminary priests, and other priests and bishops ordained by foreign authority, as did secretly before lurk in sundry parts of that Realm, do now more boldly and presumptuously show and declare themselves in the use and exercise of their functions, and in contempt of the King, his laws and religion. He has therefore thought meet to declare and publish to all his loving subjects in the Realm of Ireland his high displeasure with the report and rumour, and with the authors and spreaders thereof, and his resolve never to do any act that may confirm the hopes of any creature, that they shall ever have from him any toleration to exercise any other religion than that which is agreeable to God's Word, and is established by the laws of the Realm.'

But in one significant respect the Ulster Plantation fell short of its original intention: Ulster did not become an exclusively Protestant area. There were not quite enough settlers to populate the province completely, and so some of the native Irish were permitted to stay, as peasant labourers, or tenants, or even as minor landowners.

Thus, although a great deal of the land of Ireland changed hands, the Protestant north was still interspersed with deeply resentful native Catholics. The legacy of bitterness became a time-bomb that would explode sooner or later. Sir Arthur Chichester, who became Lord Deputy in 1605, was well aware of the problem when he wrote to Lord Salisbury, King

James's chief minister, in September 1610:

'The natives of those countries . . . are generally discontented, and repine greatly at their fortunes, and the small quantity of land left to them upon the division; especially those of the counties of Tyrone, Armagh and Coleraine, who, having reformed themselves in their habit and course of life beyond others, and the common expectation held of them, (for all that were able had put on English apparel, and promise to live in townships . . .) had assured themselves of better conditions from the King than those they lived in under their former landlords; but now they say they have not land given them, nor can they be admitted tenants, which is very grievous unto them. [I have] both studied and laboured the reformation of that people, and could have prevailed with them in any reasonable matter, though it were new unto them; but now I am discredited among them, for they have far less quantities assigned to them in those counties than in the other three. In which the Commissioners . . . were in my opinion, greatly overseen, or went not well . . . for to thrust the servitors with all the natives of a whole country which paid the King near £2,000 rent yearly, into little more than half a barony (as in Tyrone) was a great oversight, if not out of the meaning.'

Others were more sanguine, like Sir John Davies, who in 1612 wrote *A Discovery of the True Causes why Ireland was never entirely subdued.* His optimistic summing up of the Ulster Plantation makes bitterly ironic reading today:

'. . . the distribution and plantation thereof, hath been projected and prosecuted, by the special direction and care of the King himself; wherein His Majesty hath corrected the errors . . . committed by King Henry II and King John, in distributing and planting the first conquered lands. For, although there were six whole shires to be disposed, His Majesty gave not an entire country, or county, to any particular person; much less did he grant *Jura Regalia*, or any

31

extraordinary liberties. For the best British undertaker had but a proportion of 3,000 acres for himself, with power to create a manor, and hold a court baron; albeit, many of these undertakers, were of as great birth and quality, as the best adventurers in the first conquest. Again, His Majesty did not utterly exclude the natives out of this plantation, with a purpose to root them out, as the Irish were excluded out of the first English colonies; but made a mixed plantation of British and Irish, that they might grow up together in one nation; only, the Irish were in some places transplanted from the woods and mountains into the plains and open countries, that being removed (like wild fruit trees) they might grow the milder, and bear the better and sweeter fruit.

'And this truly, is the master-piece, and most excellent part of the work of reformation, and is worthy indeed of His Majesty's royal pains. For when this plantation hath taken root, and been fixed and settled but a few years, with the favour and blessing of God . . . it will secure the peace of Ireland, assure it to the Crown of England for ever; and finally, make it a civil and a rich, a mighty, and a flourishing Kingdom.'

It will secure the peace of Ireland! Today, the tragedy of Ulster inevitably invites historical justifications on both sides. What represents historic 'right' to territory? How far back in history does it go? In the early seventeenth century, the indigenous Irish population were systematically dispossessed of land they had come to consider their own. But what of the newcomers? They did not see themselves as political settlers, holding a redoubt for the English crown. They saw themselves as a distinct community: a community of pioneers who had cleared land, developed new and more efficient farming methods, brought prosperity and stability, and, above all, defended their form of faith, put down roots of their own for themselves and their families and descendants.

It is the perennial, irreconcilable historical legacy of seizure and settlement everywhere in the world, whether in Palestine, or Rhodesia, or Ulster.

The 'Protestant Massacre' and Cromwell's invasion

In Ulster, the powder-keg of bitterness exploded in 1641, in what has become enshrined in Protestant folk memory as the 'Protestant Massacre'. That was when the native Irish rose against their oppressors; and, according to the mythology of the North, the Protestant settlers were butchered in their hundreds of thousands. Serious historians now know that this is a distortion. In the first place, there were not 'hundreds of thousands' of settlers to butcher; and in the second place, a sober study of the evidence of contemporary documents concerning land changes and deaths suggests that the figures of the so-called Massacre have been wildly exaggerated. What is more, they were wildly exaggerated *at the time*, for specific propaganda purposes—to justify in advance the scale of any vengeance that might follow. All that the modern historian can reasonably say is that in 1641 the native Irish rose in rebellion, supported by the Old English who had assimilated with them and had seen their powers and privileges eroded by the episcopalian establishment; and in that rebellion, the pent-up frustrations and accumulated hatreds of the years expressed themselves, not for the first or by any means the last time, in death and destruction.

The rebellion of the 'Catholic Confederates', as they called themselves, lasted from 1641 to 1649. For a time, when King Charles I was too desperately engaged in England in the civil war with his Parliament to have resources to spare for Ireland, it looked as if the Rebellion might succeed. It was a stirring time, a time for heroic battle rhetoric, a rhetoric that sounds not unfamiliar to this day:

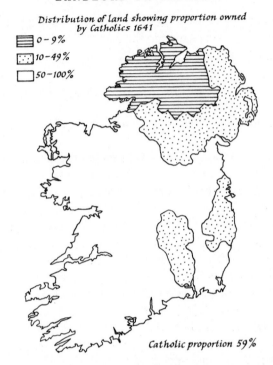

Distribution of land showing proportion owned
by Catholics 1641

▤ 0 - 9%

▦ 10 - 49%

☐ 50 - 100%

Catholic proportion 59%

'Gentlemen and Fellow Soldiers! Know that those that stand before you ready to fight are those that banished you, your Wives and Children from your Lands and Houses, and make you seek your Bread and Livelihood in strange places. Now you have Arms in your hands as good as they have, and you are Gentlemen as good as they are. You are the Flower of Ulster, descended from as Ancient and Honourable a Stock of People as any in Europe. This Land you and your Predecessors having possessed about three thousand years. All Christendom knows your quarrel is good—to Fight for your native Birthright and for the Religion which your Forefathers professed and maintained since Christianity came first to this Land.

'So as now is the time to consider your distressed and slavish condition; you have Arms in your Hands, you are as numerous as they are; and now try your Valour and your Strength on those who have banished you, and now resolve to destroy you Bud and Branch. So let your Manhood be seen by your push of Pike; and I will engage, if you do so, by God's assistance and the Intercession of His Blessed Mother and all the Holy Saints in Heaven, that the Day will be your own. Your word is *Sancta Maria*; and so in the Name of the Father, Son and Holy Ghost advance and give not Fire till you are within Pike-length.'

But the Confederates were deeply divided. The Old English were prepared to make terms with Charles in exchange for the restoration of *their* ancient privileges. The Irish Catholics, however, demanded the full recognition of Catholicism and the restoration of *all* confiscated lands. By 1649, the chance was lost. With King Charles disposed of, the English Parliament turned its full attention on Ireland, and Oliver Cromwell landed at Dublin with a Puritan army bent not only on reconquest, but on revenge. Cromwell himself described in a letter to the Council of State, dated 16 September 1649, how he dealt with the three thousand defenders of the town of Drogheda (Tredah), soon after he landed:

'Sir,

It hath pleased God to bless our endeavours at Tredah. After battery, we stormed it. The enemy were about 3,000 strong in the town. They made stout resistance, and near 1,000 of our men being entered, the enemy forced them out again. But God giving a new courage to our men, they attempted again, and entered, beating the enemy from their defences.

'The enemy had made three entrenchments, both to the right and left of where we entered; all which they were forced to quit. Being thus entered, we refused them quarter; having the day before, summoned the town. I believe we put to the sword the whole number of the defendants. I do not think thirty of the whole number escaped with their lives. Those that did, are in safe custody for Barbadoes. Since that time, the enemy quitted to us Trim and Dundalk. In Trim they were in such haste that they left their guns behind them.

'This hath been a marvellous great mercy. The enemy, being not willing to put an issue upon a field-battle, had put into this garrison almost all their prime soldiers, being about 3,000 horse and foot, under the command of their best officers; Sir Arthur Ashton being made governor. There were some seven or eight regiments, Ormond's being one, under the command of Sir Edmund Verney. I do not believe, neither do I hear, that any officer escaped with his life, save only one lieutenant, who, I hear, going to the enemy said, that he was the only man that escaped of all the garrison. The enemy were filled upon this with much terror. And truly I believe this bitterness will save much effusion of blood, through the goodness of God.

'I wish that all honest hearts may give the glory of this to God alone, to whom indeed the praise of this mercy belongs. As for instruments, they were very inconsiderable the work throughout.

'We are marching the army to Dublin, which we hope will be here tomorrow night, where we desire to recruit with victual, and shall then, God willing, advance towards the southern design . . .'

The severity and brutality of that punitive expedition has burned itself into the folk memory of the Irish Catholics, counterpointing the Protestant folk memory of the 1641 massacres, but probably with better reason. The massacre of the garrison of Wexford was one of the worst atrocities. The Governor had actually agreed surrender terms, as set out in a letter from Cromwell himself:

'Sir,
I have had the patience to peruse your propositions, to which I might have returned an answeare with some

36

disdaine. But (To bee short) I shall give the souldiers and noncommissioned officers quarter for life and leave to go to their severall habitations, with their wearing cloathes. They ingaginge themselves to live quietly there and to take upp arms no more against the Parliament of England. And the commissioned officers quarter for their lives, but to render themselves prisoners. And as for the inhabitants, I shall ingage myselfe that noe violence shall bee offered to their goods, and that I shall protect the towne from plunder.

'I expect your possetive answeare instantly and if you will upon these tearmes surrender and quitt in one houre shall send forth to mee four officers of the quality of feild officers and two Aldermen for the performance thereof I shall thereupon forbear all acts of hostility.'

What Cromwell described as 'an unexpected Providence' took place. While the negotiations were still in progress, Cromwell's troops gained access to the town, where they ran amok and began slaughtering the inhabitants. No attempt was made to check them by Cromwell himself or by any of his officers. It was a terrible blot on his career and reputation as a general.

After the rebellion had been quelled, Cromwell undertook a wholesale transfer of wealth and property from Catholics to Protestants. Landowners who had been involved in the rebellion were summarily stripped of all their estates and property rights. Landowners who had not been involved were none the less herded into a huge Catholic reservation in Connaught and Clare. The remaining counties became government property, to be parcelled out amongst the government's creditors and given to government soldiers in lieu of pay. In 1654, Vincent Gookin, the Surveyor General of Ireland, wrote prophetically:

'When will this wild war be finished; Ireland planted, inhabitants disburthened; soldiers settled? The unsettling of a nation is easy; the settling is not.'

The social patterns of Ireland had now been distorted out of all recognition. There was now a prospering Protestant upper class, and an Irish lower class of appalling degradation. Thirty years later, the English traveller Thomas Dineley in his book *Tour of Ireland*, in 1680, would paint a mournful picture:

'The descendant in a direct line from the said Earl of Desmond is said now to be a brogue maker, or maker of Irish shoes, in the county of Kerry, which, had they not forfeited their estates, as it is now worth, it is thought it would be the largest in this kingdom by 3 parts, for any particular, and at least by modest computation £200,000 per annum . . .

'The common people of both sexes wear no shoos after the English fashion, but a sort of pumps called brogues. The vulgar Irish women's garments are loose body'd without any manner of stiffening, they never wear bodys to check or direct the course of nature; having like a night cap made of a napkin about their heads instead of night geer; never at any time using hats after the manner of the vulgar English, but covering and defending their heads from rain with a mantle, as also from the heat of the sunne; to which Spanish lazy use the Irish men apply their cloaks.

'Dyet generally of the vulgar Irish are potatoes, milk, new milk, which they call sweet milk, bonny clobber, mallabaune, whey curds, large brown oatcakes of a foot and half broad bak't before the fire, bread made of bare, a sort of barley, pease, beans and oatmeale, wheat or rye for great days. Besides potatoes roasted in the embers, they feed on parsnips, carrots and watercresses. Butter, laid up in wicker basketts, buried for some time in a bog, to make a provision of an high taste for Lent. Near the shores they eat sea-weeds . . .'

--- --- Cromwell's march 1649
———— William's march 1690 –1

James II and William of Orange

After the collapse of Cromwell's Commonwealth and the Restoration of Charles II in 1660, for a time there seemed rather
better prospects for the Catholic position in Ireland—but not
as much as the Catholics hoped. For political reasons, Charles
could only make a very partial restoration of lands, for he
could not afford to offend the Parliamentary army by repeal-
ing Cromwell's land settlements wholesale. However,
Charles's reign brought a period of peace and economic
expansion for Ireland, and greater tolerance for Catholics.

The effect was simply to arouse hopes for a real Catholic revival, especially when Charles was succeeded by his Catholic

39

brother, James II. But unfortunately one man's hope is all too
often another man's despair. The more James II seemed to
favour Catholics, in England no less than in Ireland, the more
the Protestants in both countries feared for their own future.
Too many deeply vested interests were involved. Three years
after James ascended the throne, William of Orange, the
Dutch husband of James's Protestant daughter, Mary, was
invited to invade England to avert the danger of a Catholic
counter-Reformation. James fled to France; and from there,
supported by French forces, he went to Ireland, which still
looked upon him as the only hope for a Catholic nation. And
now, once again, the profoundly conflicting interests within
the divided community were set on another collision course
with disaster.

Parliament was summoned in Dublin—the so-called
'Patriot Parliament', dominated by Catholics, which sought a
greater independence from England, a total reversal of
Cromwell's land settlements, and universal freedom of conscience. Poor James, 'with his one shoe English and his one
shoe Irish', as someone put it, was caught in the cleft stick of
trying to appease both his Protestant and his Catholic subjects simultaneously. The conflicting interests were irreconcilable, and in any case the issue was about to be settled not by
debate but by force of arms. The 'War of the Two Kings', the
war between the forces of William and James, has
contributed hugely to the historical rhetoric of Protestants
and Catholics alike. For instance, there was the heroic resistance of the Derry Protestants in 1689 to the three-month
siege of their city, immortalised in the sermon preached
before the defending garrison by the Reverend Mr Seth-
whittle:

'We have been surrounded in this poor city for divers
months; beleaguer'd by a multitude of merciless and implacable enemies; exposed to danger without ceasing or
intermission. We have been deserted by those who came to

Dutch water colour painting of Irish men and women about 1575.

October 11th
1649

For the Comaund in Cheife
in the towne of Wexford

Oliver Cromwell's letter to Colonel David Sinott, commander of the Wexford garrison, setting out the terms for the surrender of Wexford.

Patrick Sarsfield, Earl of Lucan.

'King Billy' (William III).

ARTICLES

Agreed upon the Third Day of Octob.

One Thousand Six Hundred and Ninety One.

Between the Right Honourable, Sir *Charles Porter*, Knight, and *Thomas Coningsby*, Esq, Lords Justices of *Ireland*; and His Excellency the Baron *De Ginckle*, Lieutenant General, and Commander in Chief of the *English* Army ; *On the One Part* ·

And the Right Honourable, *Patrick* Earl of *Lucan*, *Percy* Viscount *Galmoy*, Colonel *Nicholas Purcel*, Colonel *Nicholas Cusack*, Sir *Toby Butler*, Colonel *Garret Dillon*, and Colonel *John Brown* ; *On the other Part :*

In the behalf of the *Irish* Inhabitants in the City and County of *Lymerick*, the Counties of *Clare*, *Kerry*, *Cork*, *Sligo*, and *Mayo*.

In Consideration of the Surrender of the City of Lymerick, *and other Agreements made between the said Lieutenant General* Ginckle, *the Governor of the City of* Lymerick, *and the Generals of the* Irish *Army, bearing Date with these Presents, for the Surrender of the said City, and Submission of the said Army : It is Agreed, That*

I.

THE *Roman Catholicks* of this Kingdom, shall enjoy such Privileges in the Exercise of their Religion, as are consistent with the Laws of *Ireland*; or as they did enjoy in the Reign of King *Charles* the II : And their Majesties, as soon as their Affairs will permit them to Summon a Parliament in this Kingdom, will endeavour to procure the said *Roman Catholicks* such farther Security in that particular, as may preserve them from any Disturbance, upon the Account of their said Religion.

First page of the Treaty of Limerick, reproduced from the articles as published officially in Dublin by the Williamite government in 1691.

our relief; tempted by parlies and specious terms of capitulation; undermined by treacherous contrivances among ourselves; exercised with all the varieties of terror and amazement.

'The small shot hath poured upon us like a shower of hail; the great guns, like thunder hath shaken our walls; and the bombs like lightning have ruin'd our houses. We have seen death in all its horrible shapes, and we are every moment entertain'd with spectacles of misery and mortality. Sickness and disease are entered within our gates, and pale famine is visible in every countenance. The fond mother hath not a morsel of bread to appease the languishing cry of her starved infant; the grateful son hath not wherewithal to sustain his aged parent.

'One friend looks at another, and sees his misery, but cannot prevent a lingring death. He that formerly had his table cover'd with variety of dishes, knows not where to satisfie nature with one wholesome bit. We cannot refresh ourselves with such scraps and morsels as we formerly allow'd our dogs; nay we are constrain'd to eat of such things, as at another time human nature would nauseate and abhor. Nevertheless God has made us this day a defenced city and an iron pillar and brazen walls against the whole land.'

In their turn, the Irish Catholics celebrate in song and story the sieges of Athlone and Limerick, and their remarkable leader, Patrick Sarsfield, Earl of Lucan; but in the demonology of Protestant history, it is the Battle of the Boyne in 1690 that has claimed the most attention, even though it did not actually end the war. Here, William of Orange with a superior force put James II to flight—right out of Ireland; and thereby the Protestant succession to the throne was assured.

But the Battle of the Boyne was more than just a straight clash between Protestants and Catholics; it was as much a battle of European power politics without religious boundaries. William, the Protestant defender, was supported by the Holy Roman Emperor and the Catholic King of Spain; while the King of France, who supported Catholic James, was at daggers drawn with the Pope!

History, especially Irish history, can seldom be fitted into neat, simplified patterns. In the Public Record Office in Belfast there hangs a painting which was believed to depict William of Orange receiving his commission from the Pope. The heretical suggestion of that painting so outraged an extremist Orangeman from Scotland that he tried to slash it to ribbons! It is ironical that recent scholarship indicates that the painting was very much later than the Battle of the Boyne and had nothing at all to do with it.

But whatever complicated patterns were created and woven in the Williamite War, one thread remains clear. Henry VIII had feared liaison between Ireland and the Continent—now 150 years later the defeated Patrick Sarsfield with 1,400 others left for France to become the forerunners of the famous 'Wild Geese', the Irish soldiers—mercenaries because they had no land or country of their own—who fought decisive battles in the European wars of the eighteenth century, and made their name at the Battle of Fontenoy. Once again, as with the 'Flight of the Earls', Ireland had lost her leaders and fighters.

PART II

The Protestant Ascendancy: 1691 - 1845

Irish History–Fact or Fiction? That is the challenging title of a recent booklet published in Ireland by the Churches Central Committee for Community Work. It was the outcome of a study of the influence of historical myths on Irish society and their emotive effect in the present situation, and it was aired at a conference entitled 'The Teaching of History—a Basis of Understanding, or a Cause of Disruption?' This conference, I may say, was attended by representatives from both the North and the South. To my mind, the mere fact that such an ecumenical conference should have been held at all in Ireland is a striking manifestation of the effect of the Historiographical Revolution. Fifty years ago, few people would even have dreamed of asking the question, never mind trying to find an answer to it.

But in the 1930s, things began to change. In 1936, two young scholars founded societies to promote the scientific study of Irish history. In Belfast, Dr T. W. Moody, later a professor at Trinity College, Dublin, formed the Ulster Society for Irish Historical Studies; and in Dublin, Dr R. Dudley Edwards, now a professor at University College, Dublin, formed the Irish Historical Society. And then, in March 1938, the two societies, led by these revolutionary young historians, started publishing a joint journal, *Irish Historical Studies*, which has been published twice a year ever since.

Before then, Irish history had usually been a form of propaganda, not to be studied but to be quarried for material with which to support entrenched and dogmatic attitudes. Now the purpose was quite simply to try to encourage proper professionalism in the study of Irish history; to try to create standards of objective research and interpretation in an area previously riddled with prejudice and sectarianism and ignorance, both in the North and the South: in a word, to try to demythologise Irish history.

It is a very slow process. It has taken a long time for the new attitudes to percolate from the universities to the outside world, where Irish history is anything but an academic subject. But it is happening. A people who, because of the peculiar pressures that their past has placed on them, might prefer to hold their historical myths inviolate, are actually beginning to ask questions like: 'Irish history—fact or fiction?'

The Popery Code

The defeat of the Catholic James II by the Protestant William of Orange at the Battle of the Boyne in 1690, and the subsequent ending of the Williamite War in Ireland by the Treaty of Limerick, was a crushing and comprehensive defeat for the Catholic cause, and it left episcopalianism firmly in the ascendancy. In the wake of their military victory, the Irish Parliament, which was entirely Protestant, set to with a will to ensure that the Protestant Ascendancy stayed. Never again must the Catholic majority be allowed to threaten the property and privileges of the ruling Protestant minority; never again must a Catholic Ireland be allowed to endanger the safety of Protestant England. To that end, the Irish Parliament, which then was entirely subordinate to the Parliament at Westminster, enacted a series of anti-Catholic laws, known as the Popery Code (or now as the Penal Laws), designed 'to prevent the further growth of Popery'.

The initiative for the sweeping provisions of the Bill of 1704 came not from Parliament at Westminster, as might have been expected, but from the Irish House of Commons, who were indeed distinctly worried that Westminster might tone them down. They were a blatant violation of the so-called 'Articles of Limerick', the terms of surrender granted to the Catholic supporters of James II in the city of Limerick and elsewhere in 1691. The very first of these Articles had promised that Irish Catholics should 'enjoy such privileges in the exercise of their religion as are consistent with the laws of Ireland, or as they did enjoy in the reign of Charles II'. The new laws were specifically designed to do away with these promised rights and to degrade the Catholic majority yet further—and in particular, to emasculate the remnants of the Catholic landed gentry:

'Whereas it is notoriously known that the late rebellions in this kingdom have been contrived, promoted and carried on by Popish archbishops, bishops, Jesuits and other ecclesiastical persons of the Romish clergy. And forasmuch as the peace and publick safety of the kingdom is in danger, by the great number of the said archbishops which, not only endeavour to withdraw His Majesty's subjects from their obedience, but do daily stir up and move sedition and rebellion . . .

No Catholic may sit in the Irish Parliament.

No Catholic may be a solicitor, game-keeper or constable.

No Catholic may possess a horse of greater value than £5. Any Protestant offering that sum can take possession of the hunter or carriage horse of his Roman Catholic neighbour.

No Catholic may attend a university, keep a school, or send his children to be educated abroad. £10 reward is offered for the discovery of a Roman Catholic schoolmaster.

No Catholic may buy land or receive it as a gift from a Protestant.

45

No Catholic may bequeath his estate as a whole, but must divide it among all his sons, unless one of those sons become Protestant, where he will inherit the whole estate.

No Catholic may be the guardian of a child. The orphan children of Catholics must be brought up as Protestants.'

And this is a summary of only some of the Penal Laws. No Catholic could hold a commission in the armed forces, or sit on the Bench, or hold any government office at all. Catholics were debarred from standing for Parliament; they didn't even have a vote. The Catholic Church itself was proscribed, as were Catholic pilgrimages. The whole point and purpose of this penal legislation was to keep the Catholics in permanent subjection to a Protestant minority. For instance, the clause about not owning a horse worth more than £5 was designed to prevent the possibility of Catholics ever again building up a cavalry force. The clause on divided inheritance was designed to make it virtually impossible for a Catholic ever to become a major landowner. The total burden of the Popery Code was aimed at preventing the emergence of an educated, or professional, or landed, Catholic leadership. In the face of this relentless pressure, many notable Catholic landlords and lawyers abandoned their old religion and went over to the established church, the episcopalian Church of Ireland. By the end of the eighteenth century, scarcely five per cent of Irish land was owned by Catholics.

Curiously enough, it was not only the Catholics in Ireland who were profoundly disadvantaged by the Popery Code. The English Privy Council, for some obscure reason, took it upon itself to insert into the 1704 Act designed 'to prevent the further growth of Popery' a sacramental test aimed against the Protestant Dissenters in Ireland—most of whom were Presbyterians. This excluded from offices of trust or profit under the crown all those who had not taken Communion according to the rites of the Established Church of Ireland. This effectively disenfranchised Ulster Presbyterians from both

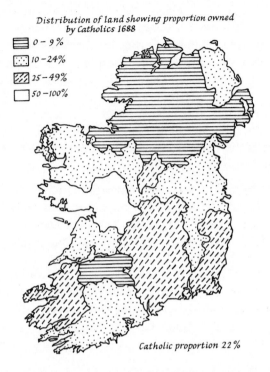

Distribution of land showing proportion owned
by Catholics 1688

- 0 – 9 %
- 10 – 24 %
- 25 – 49 %
- 50 – 100 %

Catholic proportion 22 %

Parliament and the corporations of Belfast and Londonderry, where they had previously been in control. These sanctions applied to Dissenters throughout most of the eighteenth century, and would play a significant role in the mass emigrations from Ulster in the second half of the century.

On the surface, however, the professed aim of the Penal Laws was to extirpate the Catholic religion in Ireland, root and stock and branch; but little attempt was made to enforce that particular aspect. It was power, not piety, that was at stake. Hundreds of priests had been banished, under threat of death for high treason; but by the middle of the eighteenth century, the Catholic Church was back at full strength—even though it officially had no churches. The Protestant authorities increasingly turned a blind eye on the innumerable makeshift chapels in which Catholic worship was openly conducted. Stables or storehouses were the usual venues, but if no buildings were available, masses for the peasantry were held in the open air, in the lee of hedgerows—'hedge-masses', as they came to be called. Despite the apparent severity of the statutes, some Protestant landowners proved to be astonishingly tolerant. It is reported that a prominent local squire in Fermanagh, Sir John Caldwell, was particularly considerate to the wretched peasants huddling under the hedges for their devotions:

> '. . . although a staunch Protestant, [he] always treated the Roman Catholics with humanity and tenderness; in particular, one stormy day, when it rained very hard, he discovered a priest, with his congregation, at mass under a hedge; and, instead of taking that opportunity of blaming them for thus meeting so near his house (and having the priest hung, as he might have done), he ordered his cows to be driven out of a neighbouring cow-house, and signified to the priest and people, that they might there take shelter from the weather, and there finish their devotions in peace.'

The Peasantry

For all the Catholic peasantry life has been painted as having been uniformly wretched. Certainly poverty was endemic in many areas, and getting worse as the population increased. But this poverty apparently was not a direct consequence of the Penal Laws, which were not really directed at the peasants anyway, for they had neither property nor power. The peasant did not much care whether his landlord was Catholic or Protestant—only that the rent seemed to be rising all the time. In October 1703, Colonel Henry Conyngham in Dublin wrote a fairly typical letter to Lady Murray, in Wigtownshire, complaining of the shortage of money in Ireland, especially among his tenants in County Donegal, and announcing his purchase of a more profitable estate in County Meath:

> 'If this kingdom continues in the miserable degree of poverty it now labours under, nobody can expect rents in money, and what is worse, all commodities are at so very low a rate that, even in commodities, tenants will not be able to discharge half the rents they are set at, and for the future, till the world mend, I can promise you nothing but such distresses as the land I hold from you affords . . .'

One contributory factor to the parlous state of the Irish economy at this time was the English 'Woollen Act' of 1699. This prohibited the export overseas of all woollen cloth from Ireland, and placed a penal tariff on woollen imports into England. It was a frankly protectionist measure, pushed through by the West Country cloth lobby, to shield England's most important export. The effect was to sabotage this new and growing part of the Irish economy, particularly in the south, before it had a chance to become a properly established industry—as it had every likelihood of doing, because the cost of labour and other overheads were much lower than in England. Modern historians now tend to think that the damaging effects of the 1699 Woollen Act were exaggerated by eighteenth-century pamphleteers for political purposes; but there is no mistaking the despairing note in a letter from Cork (the region most affected by the Act) by Sir Thomas Southwell, one of the Commissioners of the Irish Revenue, to his father-in-law, Lord Coningsby, Vice-Treasurer for Ireland, in August 1699:

> 'Here is no news from this place but the deplorable condition of many families that are starving, who were concerned in the bays [woollen cloth] trade, and all of them English, they being the only people of this nation ruined by that act, and made a scorn to the Scots and Irish. 300 families left this city last week and embarked for Holland,

in order to go to Sweedland [Sweden], where they say they have great encouragement. There are 800 gone in all from about this city, Tallow, Bandon, Midleton and Youghal, so that there are no common English left in this country at all, which was the only place like an English plantation in Ireland. What will be the consequence of it, God knows.'

It was the conditions of the poor in southern Ireland that provoked Jonathan Swift, Dean of St Patrick's Cathedral in Dublin, into one of his most savage satires against the Establishment. In *A Modest Proposal for Preventing the Children of Ireland from being a Burden to their Parents or Country*, published in 1729, he blandly suggested that they should be—eaten:

'I have been assured by a very knowing American of my acquaintance in London, that a young, healthy child well nursed, is, at a year old, a most delicious, nourishing and wholesome food, whether stewed, roasted, baked or boiled; and I make no doubt that it will equally serve in a fricassee, or a ragout.'

With unwitting irony, actual famine struck in 1741—an ominous augury of the catastrophe of the Great Famine that would devastate the population a century later. Travellers who wrote about the Irish peasantry in the second half of the eighteenth century constantly remarked on their squalid surroundings. Arthur Young, for instance, who enjoyed a European reputation as an agricultural expert, visited the country in the 1770s and wrote about the peasantry in *A Tour in Ireland*:

'The cottages of the Irish, which are called cabbins, are the most miserable looking hovels that can well be conceived ... The furniture of the cabbins is as bad as the architecture; in very many consisting only of a pot for boiling their potatoes, a bit of a table, and one or two broken stools; beds are not found universally, the family lying on straw.'

Similarly, the French traveller known as Le Chevalier de La Tocnaye who published *A Frenchman's Walk through Ireland*:

> 'Half a dozen children, almost naked, were sleeping on a little straw with a pig, a dog, a cat, two chickens and a duck. The poor woman spread a mat on a chest, the only piece of furniture in the house, and invited me to lie there. The animals saluted the first ray of the sun by their cries and began to look about for something to eat. The dog came to smell me; the pig put up her snout at me and began to grunt; the chickens and the duck began to eat my powder bag, and the children began to laugh. I got up very soon for fear of being devoured. I should add that I had no small difficulty in making my hostess accept a shilling.'

Poor, fastidious M. Le Chevalier! It is a vivid little cameo, and I am not the first person to be unable to resist the temptation of including it. However, it illustrates the danger of using memorable quotations selectively while making generalisations about a whole country for a whole century. Even that eminently respectable contemporary source, Arthur Young, went on to say:

> '. . . the exceptions are very numerous. I have been in a multitude of cabbins that had much useful furniture, and some even superfluous; chairs, tables, boxes, chests of drawers, earthen ware, and in short most of the articles found in a middling English cottage; but, upon enquiry, I very generally found that these acquisitions were all made within the last ten years; a sure sign of a rising national prosperity.'

But there was one ominously significant and prophetic section in Arthur Young's book: his description of the fecundity of the Irish peasantry, and the conditions that would help to create a population explosion that would leave Ireland so vulnerable to the catastrophe of the Potato Famine in the 1840s, when the population had soared to eight million people:

'The cabbins of the poor Irish, being such apparently miserable habitations, is another very evident encouragement to population. In England, where the poor are in many respects in such a superior state, a couple will not marry unless they can get a house, to build which . . . will cost from twenty-five to sixty pounds; half the life, and all the vigour and youth of a man and woman are passed, before they can save such a sum . . . But in Ireland the cabbin is not an object of a moment's consideration; to possess a cow and a pig is an earlier aim; the cabbin begins with a hovel, that is erected with two days' labour; and the young couple pass not their youth in celibacy for want of a nest to produce their young in . . .

'Marriage is certainly more general in Ireland than in England: I scarce ever found an unmarried farmer or cottar; but it is seen more in other classes, which with us do not marry at all; such as servants; the generality of footmen and maids, in gentlemen's families, are married, a circumstance we very rarely see in England.

'Another point of importance is their children not being burthensome. In all the enquiries I made into the state of the poor, I found their happiness and ease generally relative to the number of their children, and nothing considered as such a misfortune as having none; whenever this is the fact, or the general idea, it must necessarily have a considerable effect in promoting early marriages, and consequently population.

'The food of the people being potatoes is a point not of less importance; for when the common food of the poor is so dear as to be an object of attentive economy, the children will want that plenty which is essential to rearing them; the article of milk, so general in the Irish cabbins, is a matter of the first consequence in rearing infants. The Irish poor in the Catholick parts of that country are subsisted entirely upon land; whereas the poor in England have so little to do with it, that they subsist almost entirely from shops, by a purchase of their necessaries . . . Generally speaking the Irish poor have a fair belly-full of potatoes, and they have milk the greatest part of the year.'

It is observations such as those that can illuminate the course of Irish history for us more usefully than the generality of patriotic rodomontade. Irish history has for too long been exclusively concerned with the politics of violence and op-pression, with heroes and villains, with sweeping rhetorical generalisations. There is still a tremendous amount of work to be done in studying the social, economic and farming history of Ireland, and also its rich cultural history—not always ex-clusively Irish but often the outcome of fecund fertilisation from other cultures. There is a present lack, too, of micro-history—the study of individual communities, particular localities, specific parishes. Only in that way will a reliable picture of eighteenth-century Ireland be built up. And it may help to explain why one Catholic scholar I met in Dublin thinks that the eighteenth century in Ireland was an un-usually pleasant century; with settlers and natives living to-gether in reasonable harmony, with the middle classes reasonably prosperous, and with the peasantry reasonably serene.

Ireland and America

There is one fact about eighteenth-century Ireland, however, that cannot be challenged, and which needs expla-nation—the fact that in a largely Protestant Ulster there was so much social discontent that in the second half of the century more than a quarter of a million Ulster Presbyte-rians uprooted themselves and emigrated to America. How-

ever bad the conditions in Ulster may have been, they could
not have been as harrowing as the conditions on the emigrant
ships. This is how one John Smilie described his long journey
across the Atlantic in a letter to his father, dated 11 November
1762:

'We had a Wind, Father, which drove us so far North,
that our Weather became extremely cold, with much Rain
and hard Gales of Wind. Yet in the midst of all our Mise-
ries, our Captain showed not the least Remorse or Pity. We
had our full Allowance of Bread and Water only for the first
Fortnight. Then we were reduced to three Pints per day,
and three Pounds and a Half per Week. On the twelfth of
July we espied a Mountain of Ice of prodigious Size. On the
thirteen, Father, our Weather became more moderate (but
very foggy).

'August the first, our Weather became extremely warm,
and the Crew of Passengers very weak. We had Beef, but
could make no Use of it, for Thirst; for we were a Week that
we had but half a Pint of Water per Day for each Person.
The tenth Day, Father, our Allowance of Bread came to
two Pounds and a Half per week to each Passenger. Next
week we had only one Pound and a Half. Since the Time of
our setting sail, we lost sixty-four of our Crew by Death,
and the next twelve Days we lived upon two Biscuits and a
half for that Time, and a half a Naggin of Barley each,
which we ate raw, for want of Water to boil it in.

'Hunger and Thirst, Father, had now reduced our Crew
to the last Extremity. Nothing was now to be heard aboard
our Ship but the Cries of distressed children, and of their
distressed Mothers, unable to relieve them. Our ship now
was truly a real Spectacle of Horror! Never a Day passed
without one or two of our Crew put over Board. Many kill'd
themselves by drinking Salt Water; and their own Urine
was a common Drink.

'We were now out of Hope of ever seeing land. August

the twenty-ninth we had only one Pint of Water for each Person, which was all we Passengers would have got: and our Bread was done. But on that Day, August the twenty-ninth, the Lord was pleased to send the greatest Shower of Rain I ever saw, which was the Means of preserving our Lives. After this, tho' we had no bread, yet, we thought, we lived well.

'You may judge of Captain Taylor's Character by this, that, notwithstanding all the Straits we were in for Bread and Water, neither he, nor his Mistress, nor five others that were his Favourites, ever came to Allowance. We had fair Winds, Father, and, for most Part, Rains every Day. On the first of September we sounded, and found ourselves in forty Fathom Water; and the next morning—about eight o'clock—we saw Land. On Sunday Morning, the fourth of September—to the inexpressible Joy of all our Ship's Crew of Passengers—we came to an Anchor off Newcastle: so that we had a Passage of fourteen weeks and five days.'

Perhaps what provoked young men like John Smilie to leave was a pent-up frustration with the religious intolerance of the Penal Laws that made them, too, as Presbyterians, second-class citizens compared with the episcopalian adherents of the established Church of Ireland. Perhaps they had heard of America as the land of opportunity and freedom. Certainly when they arrived there, they found themselves in the midst of electrifying political events that were to have a profound influence on Irish politics—the American War of Independence in the 1770s.

The American colonies and Ireland had much in common within the British imperial framework, particularly in the legislative field, for Westminster claimed the right to legislate for them both, despite their own representative assemblies. And now the American colonists were showing the new immigrants that it was not only desirable, but eminently possible, to defy the British Parliament and achieve independence. Nor was it a simple question of nationalism; throughout the century, Westminster had placed severe restraints on Irish trade in order to protect English industries, just as it had controlled the trade of the American colonies.

Yet despite all the economic restrictions, Ireland's prosperity had actually been increasing. In the north, the linen industry was flourishing and Belfast was growing fast. In the south, improved returns from agriculture were enabling the landed gentry to increase their rents. Ireland was doing quite well—and as a consequence, no doubt, wanted to do a lot better. The example of the American colonists promptly galvanised political activity in Dublin. Concurrently, the British government was in serious trouble. France and Spain had joined the American War of Independence on the American side in 1778, and the standing army in Ireland had been despatched to America as reinforcements. Mindful of the danger of foreign invasion, Irish Protestants formed groups of Volunteers all over the country, which soon became political pressure groups. The time was ripe for concessions.

To conciliate the Irish Protestants, the British government abolished the trade restrictions; and then, as the American war situation worsened, a new government allowed greater legislative freedom to the Irish Parliament. Some relief for the Catholics was also imperative. For some years there had been a growing conviction amongst enlightened Catholics and Protestants alike that there should be an oath of allegiance which would separate loyal and well-affected Catholics from the disaffected—some formula, acceptable both to the government and the Catholic conscience, which would allow the Irish Catholics to reassure the government of their loyalty without abjuring their religion.

Such an oath was incorporated in an Act of the Irish Parliament in 1774, and many Catholics, both laymen and clergy, took it. But there was no immediate relaxation of the Penal Laws. In 1778, however, the first of the Catholic Relief Acts extended significant benefits to those Catholics who took the new oath. Catholic Relief was obviously long overdue; and when the Bill was sent over from Ireland, the British Attorney-General, Alexander Wedderburn, and the Solici-tor-General, James Wallace, underlined in a report to the Privy Council the degrading iniquity of the Penal Laws as they stood:

> 'The two acts of Queen Anne deprive every Papist of the common rights of a subject in the acquisition, enjoyment and disposition of property, and the natural rights of a parent in the administration of his family concerns. The ex-ecution of this law is not left to the care of government, but by a policy more ingenious than laudable, it is secured by exciting the activity of informers and by holding out temp-tations to those relations who are disposed to attack each other . . .'

Grattan's Parliament

The Irish politician whose name is most closely associated with this period of wringing concessions from England and of beginning the destruction of the humiliating and demoralising Penal Laws was Henry Grattan, a young Protestant barrister from Dublin. He quickly became the most respected leader of the liberalising reform movement, and the Parliament whose legislative independence from Westminster he temporarily ac-complished in 1782 is familiarly, if inaccurately, known as 'Grattan's Parliament'. He was apparently a superb Parlia-mentarian, a magnificent orator whose impassioned pleas for legislative independence with dignity had a tremendous effect both on public opinion and on governmental circles. It was true that the first moves for emancipation of the Catholics in 1778 had come not from Grattan's coterie but from Lord North's ministry in London, which had less motive for hos-tility to the Irish Catholics—instinctive enemies of the extreme revolutionaries in America who invoked the memory of William III's Glorious Revolution of 1688—than had the

Irish Protestant episcopalians, many of whom feared that any concession to the Catholics would prove the first snowfall of an avalanche bearing away the lands whose confiscation had so benefited their ancestors. Grattan really was, for his time, exceptionally liberal in the matter of religious tolerance, or as liberal as it was possible to be. However, a speech he made to members of the episcopalian Protestant Ascendancy in Dublin illustrates just how narrow were the bounds of liberalism in the political context of that period:

> 'I love the Roman Catholic. I am a friend to his liberty, but it is only inasmuch as his liberty is entirely consistent with your ascendancy, and addition to the strength and freedom of the Protestant community.'

Grattan seemed to be enormously successful. He achieved, for a time, an independent *parliament*, but he failed to achieve an independent *government*. He envisaged an ideal Protestant nation that contained free and happy Catholics, an independent nation in partnership with England, sharing the same monarchy. But events were to prove that this was a political chimera—a gentlemen's agreement to consolidate the power of the Protestant Ascendancy without satisfying the very different political aspirations of the population at the grass roots. Within twenty years, everything that Grattan thought he had achieved had vanished and Ireland was even less independent, if that were possible, than she had ever been before—because now events in France overtook the fortunes of Grattan and Ireland.

Wolfe Tone and the 1798 Rebellion

We must never forget how much Ireland's history is part and parcel of European history. The outbreak of the French Revolution in 1789, and the overthrow of the ruling classes there, exhilarated radical-minded liberals everywhere—especially when the new French Republic offered to help any small nation which was oppressed. In the face of this threat, Grattan's Irish Establishment closed ranks with the English once again.

In Ireland, one of those most influenced by the heady prospects of total independence and social revolution—and, be it said, disillusioned by what he thought was Grattan's limited political vision—was another young Protestant Dublin barrister, Theobald Wolfe Tone. In some ways, he might be called the first Irish Nationalist proper. In 1791, Wolfe Tone founded in both Belfast and Dublin a movement called the United Irishmen. Its object was to get rid of English influence once and for all:

> 'Our provinces are ignorant of each other, uncemented like the image which Nebuchadnezzar saw, with a head of fine gold, legs of iron and feet of clay, parts that do not cleave together—we must unite them. That is our end. The Rights of Man in Ireland, the greatest happiness of the greatest number in this island.'

The movement had to be a secret one, for it quickly became apparent that reform would not come through peaceful persuasion, but would eventually have to be carried by armed force, as had happened in France and America. The Irish themselves were no strangers to secrecy and conspiratorial societies in the eighteenth century, as peasant resentment over their conditions turned to organised militancy. Riots flared. Catholics and Protestants fought for the possession of land culminating in 1795 in the celebrated 'Battle of the Diamond' (a village near Loughgall in southern Ulster), where at least thirty people were killed. It was after that particular encounter that the victorious Protestants met in the smoking ruins of a cottage and formed a new society to defend their religion and their land against the Catholics. Thus was the Orange Order founded.

Wolfe Tone and his United Irishmen were running into trouble by now. In the first place, the name of the movement was more optimistic than realistic: the Irishmen were *not* united. Wolfe Tone himself was a republican, as were the radical Protestant liberals of Belfast. The Catholics were not; and they had been astutely appeased by the British government by a limited granting of the vote in 1793. They were still debarred from Parliament, from the Bench, and from the higher offices of State; but at least it was something. In the second place, the secrecy of the United Irishmen had been 'blown', as the phrase goes, and the British government forces were hunting down the ringleaders. The fact that the United Irishmen were also actively seeking armed help from France made them all vulnerable to charges of treason.

Wolfe Tone himself had gone to France in 1796 for help, and in December of that year he set sail from Brest on board an invasion fleet of forty-three French ships with 15,000 picked troops. Britain, at war with France, tried to blockade the port and failed; but the French fleet was scattered by winter storms, and was unable to rendezvous at Bantry Bay. The British government had had a narrow escape, and now, in real alarm, it started a series of systematic raids to disarm Ulster. By 1798, the leaders of the United Irishmen felt they had no choice: with or without French help, they would have to launch their rebellion before they were picked off one by one. But by now their organisation was so disorganised that the insurrection was sporadic, an unco-ordinated series of local risings in the north and the south. In the north, there were risings in County Antrim and County Down; in the south, in the counties of Wexford and Waterford. The authorities were desperately worried, not only by the savagery displayed by the rebels but by the possibility of defections by Catholic militiamen in the government forces. John Beresford, the Chief Commissioner of the Revenue, Dublin, expressed the dilemma in a letter to Lord Auckland dated 8 June 1798; this was three days after a government garrison of 2,000 troops had successfully defended the town of New Ross, County Wexford, against a rebel army of some 20,000 men.

'It appears that these men, inflamed by their priests, who accompany them in their ranks, fight with a mad desperation. It is becoming too apparent that this is to be a religious bloody war. We must conceal it as long as we can, because a great part of our army, and most of our militia, are papists; but it cannot be long concealed. To the murders they commit on unarmed Protestants is added the horror of their shooting many of their Protestant prisoners . . .

'This circumstance of a religious war must urge most strongly the necessity of sending as many men over as is possible, and, if necessary, passing an act through both Houses, in a day, to authorise the sending of such militia and yeomen as will voluntarily come; for if the militia should turn, or the French come, before the contest is ended and the rebellion crushed, Ireland goes first, and Great Britain follows, and all Europe after . . .'

Help from France, when it came, was too little and too late. A small force of 1,000 men landed at Killala Bay in north-east Mayo on 23 August 1798. By then, the most threatening phase of the Rebellion, the Wexford rising, was over. The French failed to find adequate local support; they were overwhelmed by superior forces at Ballinamuck, County Leitrim, on September 8, and surrendered.

Then came the *coup de grâce*. A small French squadron sailing for the north coast was captured by British naval vessels. Wolfe Tone was discovered aboard, wearing a French uniform. He was found guilty of treason by a court martial in Dublin, but before he could be executed he committed suicide in his cell on 19 November 1798. The 1798 Rebellion was over.

It had been, by any objective standards, a total and tragic failure. It had not achieved any of its objectives: independence as a republic, full civil and political rights for all, equality for all, and the abolition of all religious discrimination. Indeed, the one immediate effect it did have ran directly counter to all its objectives; because now the British Prime Minister, William Pitt the Younger, realised that Ireland was such an intractable political and strategic problem that it could only be resolved by a fundamental rethinking of Ireland's relationship with Britain. The answer, he decided, was a union of the British and Irish Parliaments.

The Act of Union, 1800

However unpalatable it might be to many Irishmen, it was a bold and imaginative proposal, which Pitt had been nursing for several years. Pitt was planning to create a British Common Market, in effect, in which Ireland would benefit by being involved in a huge free trade area with the richest empire in the world, thereby helping to raise Irish living standards all round, attract British capital investment in Irish industry, and mollify the minority fears about Catholic emancipation (which Pitt himself favoured) by making the Protestants a majority within the United Kingdom, as opposed to a minority within Ireland. But unpalatable it proved to be. In 1799, Pitt's proposal was rejected by the Irish Parliament by five votes. One member described in a letter the passions aroused amongst the opposition:

'The most popular and applauded speeches on the nights of the debate here were those of the lawyers who denied the competence of Parliament, who insisted that if the measure passed it was as a law null and void—that the people were not bound to obey and that they had a *right* to *resist*. A lieutenant-colonel of militia said that if it passed he should thereby hold himself absolved from his oath of allegiance . . .

'Certain people are doing everything in their power to bind the opposition into one firm body. If they succeed, the government here cannot stand it.'

Viscount Castlereagh, Chief Secretary for Ireland, confided to Earl Camden, the former Lord Lieutenant, his views about the extraordinary amount of political bribery and patronage that would be required to obtain a majority for the Union proposal:

'. . . You can easily imagine the complicated negotiations of private objects we are at present incessantly engaged in. Every individual is now playing his game as if it was his last stake, and it is most difficult to meet their expectations in any degree, keeping within the possibility of accomplishment. You must be prepared for having the favours and patronage of the crown most deeply engaged to the actors in this contest. I wish much to see Mr Pitt on this subject and to know distinctly what his ideas are—what lengths he is prepared to go to carry this measure.

'In England a measure may be carried by public opinion against the private inclinations of the Parliament; but here not. Besides we cannot hope that the public will do more than consent. It will ultimately, rely on it, be brought to a private question. Those who thrive by the game of Parliament are in general in their hearts against it, and unless connected with their own aggrandisement in some shape will either oppose it or give it but a languid support which encourages opposition in others . . .

'The measure may be carried, and I have no doubt will in course of time, by its own intrinsic merits. But it deserves to be considered that, if its accomplishment is delayed for any length of time by an endeavour to economise the favours of the crown, exclusive of the risk which may arise from unforeseen events there is reason to apprehend that government may be driven to the necessity of conferring those favours beforehand which have now been held out as contingent on the event: the consequence of which must be additional weakness and a future increase of the evil which is attempted to be avoided.

'. . . Mr Pitt, if he feels the Union indispensable to the Empire and to his government, must be prepared to make great sacrifices and must yield to what he would naturally wish to resist. And if he feels as strongly upon it as I conceive from the nature of the object he must do, I am inclined to think he will consider that no effort ought to be neglected which is not inconsistent with the future constitution of the Empire.'

Modern historians tend to play down the traditional nationalist view that the Union was only passed by means of massive corruption; instead, they emphasise the importance of economic and regional considerations in swaying parliamentary opinion. But the fact remains that the lengths Pitt was prepared to go to carry 'this measure' were quite considerable, in terms of political patronage—namely, 28 life peerages, 7 earldoms, 7 viscountcies, 3 marquisates, and 2 bishoprics. The Act of Union was passed in the summer of 1800, and on 1 January 1801 Ireland became part of the United Kingdom. The Lord Lieutenant, Marquess Cornwallis, duly congratulated the assembled Houses of Parliament in Dublin on 2 August 1800:

'. . . I am persuaded that the great Measure which is now accomplished could never have been effected but by a decided Conviction on your Part that it would tend to restore and to preserve the Tranquillity of this Country, to increase its Commerce and Manufactures, to perpetuate its Connexion with Great Britain, and to Augment the Resources of the Empire; you will not fail to impress these Sentiments on the Minds of your Fellow Subjects; you will encourage and improve that just Confidence which they have manifested in the Result of your Deliberations on this arduous Question; above all, you will be studious to inculcate the full Conviction, that, united with the People of Great Britain into one Kingdom, governed by the same

Sovereign, protected by the same Laws, and represented in the same Legislature, nothing will be wanting on their Part but a Spirit of Industry and Order to insure to them the full Advantages under which the People of Great Britain have enjoyed a greater Degree of Prosperity, Security and Freedom than has ever yet been experienced by any other Nation.'

The Campaign for Catholic Emancipation

In the early days of the Union the most pressing issue was the question of full emancipation for the Catholics. Most of the Penal Laws had been repealed by then, but Catholics still could not sit in Parliament or hold high offices of State in law or the Army. Pitt had virtually promised to remove the remaining restrictions at the time of the Union proposals, but as soon as the Union came into effect, he was forced to abandon the promise in the face of absolute opposition from King George III. Pitt resigned in consequence, for a time, and circulated a manifesto to Irish Catholic leaders in which he sought to justify his conduct. He called on them to remain calm, and to accept that Catholic Emancipation could not be carried for the time being. He did not, however, admit publicly that in an effort to calm the 'poor mad King's' agitated mind, he had pledged himself never again to introduce Catholic Emancipation during the King's lifetime.

'Mr Pitt's Manifesto' was bitterly attacked in an article in the *Morning Chronicle* of 12 March 1801:

'There are some expressions in this singular communication which leave the character and views of the new administration, and the relations existing between them and the old, extremely doubtful. *Many who remain in office are to give their support to the Catholic question*, but Mr Pitt cannot "concur in a hopeless attempt *to force it now*".

65

What is the meaning of this? Is it intended to reconcile the Catholics to a juggle similar to that which Mr Pitt practised when Earl Fitzwilliam was recalled from Ireland? Mr Pitt will not give his support to the question *now*. Does he wish to amuse the Catholics, to renounce the pledge he had given them? Does he hope to prevail on them to invest *him* with their confidence, and to rely upon *him* to choose the time when there will be no occasion to make "a hopeless attempt to force the question"? We do suspect something like such a proceeding. We see the usual characteristics of Mr Pitt's policy. He wants to get the first anxiety and hope of the Catholics obviated. He wishes to bring them to dependence on him. He wishes to cajole them to appoint him the arbiter of their fate. He would redeem the pledge to the Catholics as he did to those who foolishly relied on him on the question of parliamentary reform. The Catholics should remember this part of Mr Pitt's public life. They will then know how far prospects from that quarter are to be compared with those from any other. Mr Pitt may be elevated to power by the intrigue he is agitating! But will the Catholics gain their objects? The Catholics may rely on Mr Pitt "establishing their cause in the public favour; that he will give it his zealous support when it can be given with a prospect of success". But when are these happy moments to arrive? *Rusticus expectat dum defluat amnis.*

'We will venture to say that never did there issue from the pen of any man a paper so treacherous to the King, so disrespectful to Parliament and to the country, as Mr Pitt's manifesto. It marks a thirst of power so unbounded, a spirit of faction and cabal so dangerous, and withal a conduct with regard to the Catholic body so delusive, that we cannot think any set of men in the nation can read without indignation. It is equally disgraceful to the man who professes loyalty to his sovereign, affection for his country and good faith towards those whose confidence he solicits.'

66

Catholic Emanicipation became the slogan of the hour. One MP, Lord Robert Fitzgerald, the Member for County Kildare, took a cynically pragmatic view in a letter to his brother, the Duke of Leinster, in August 1802:

'I am, you know, decidedly friendly to the question of *complete* Catholic Emancipation. Indeed, I go further. I would have that sect taken entirely out of the hands of foreign powers, and I would have them liberally paid by our own government. In a word, I would do everything for them that could tend to weaken the venom of their sting, for in matters of religion nothing irritates more than opposition, and there cannot be a doubt that the poison exists still in all its virulence.

'As for the religion itself, I abhor it. It is dangerous, un-natural and highly mischievous, and I think there is much to be apprehended from the temper and designs of its preachers. But on that very account, I would not drive it to despair and provoke it, and I act from a principle of self-defence when I say that I would grant everything to the professors of that religion which could tend to remove the grounds of irritation and weaken its active spirit.

'When there is an object in view, whether that object is worth attaining or not, it is in the nature of man to pursue it through every extremity, and I am persuaded that those men will never rest till they have gained their point, and while that is the case, there can be no lasting security for Ireland.'

A notable opponent of any concessions to the Catholics, John Foster, formerly Speaker of the Irish House of Commons, compiled in February 1803 a summary of the provisions of all Acts passed in the reign of George III for the relief of Irish Catholics—no doubt to show that no further measures were necessary. It gives a telling insight into the minds of the opponents of Catholic Emancipation at the time.

The 1793 Act represented the position in Ireland at the time of the Union:

'Anno 33 geo. III (1793) Chapter 21: An act for the relief of his Majesty's Popish or Roman Catholic subjects of Ireland. This act sweeps away almost every remaining disqualification which would affect his Majesty's subjects of this persuasion. For by it the former oath of allegiance is altered and adapted to their profession; the abjuration oath and declarations formerly required, and the test of receiving the sacrament according to the Established Church, are there repealed and they are by this act qualified for every office, civil or military, may vote at elections, may be on the commission of the peace and hold any office of trust, except such as relate to the ecclesiastical establishment. And excepting also their voting in Parliament or filling a few of the great offices of state—such as being Lord Lieutenant or Lord Deputy etc, Secretaries of State, members of Privy Council, Lord High Chancellor, Lord Chief Justices, the judges in the course of law, Prime Serjeant, Attorney- and Solicitor-General, second and third Serjeants at law, King's Counsel, Masters in Chancery, Provost or fellows of Trinity College, Postmaster-General, generals on the staff, governor, sheriff, or sub-sheriff of any county—excepting these and a few similar which can only affect a very few individuals, the Roman Catholics of Ireland have every privilege and enjoyment the same as their Protestant fellow-subjects.'

Across the water, the Reverend Sydney Smith, the English journalist and wit who was co-founder of the influential *Edinburgh Review*, brought to the question of Catholic Emancipation the full range of his scathing polemic:

'Nothing is said or thought of the enormous risk to which Ireland is exposed—nothing of the gross injustice with which the Catholics are treated—nothing of the lucrative

68

apostasy of those from whom they experience this treatment: but the only concern by which we all seem to be agitated is, that the King must not be vexed in his old age. We have a great respect for the King; and wish him all the happiness compatible with the happiness of his people. But these are not times to pay foolish compliments to kings, or the sons of kings, or to anybody else: this journal has always preserved its character for courage and honesty; and it shall do so to the last . . .

'Lord Hawkesbury says that nothing is to be granted to the Catholics from fear. What! not even justice? . . .

'The moment the very name of Ireland is mentioned, the English seem to bid adieu to common feeling, common prudence and common sense, and to act with the barbarity of tyrants and the fatuity of idiots . . .

'If you tie your horse up to a gate, and beat him cruelly, is he vicious because he kicks you? If you have plagued and worried a mastiff dog for years, is he mad because he flies at you whenever he sees you? Hatred is an active, troublesome passion. Depend upon it, whole nations have always some reason for their hatred. Before you refer the turbulence of the Irish to incurable defects in their character, tell me if you have treated them as friends and equals? Have you protected their commerce? Have you respected their religion? Have you been as anxious for their freedom as your own? Nothing of all this.'

Sydney Smith reserved his richest wrath for the curious system whereby Catholics were forced to pay tithes, not to their own church, but to the established episcopalian Church of Ireland—the Church of the Protestant Ascendancy.

'In a parish where there are four thousand Catholics and fifty Protestants, the Protestants may meet together in a vestry meeting, at which no Catholic has the right to vote, and tax all the lands in the parish 1/6d. per acre, or in the pound, I forget which, for the repairs of the church—and

how has the necessity of these repairs been ascertained? A
Protestant plumber has discovered that it wants new leading; a Protestant carpenter is convinced the timbers are not
sound, and the glazier who hates holy water (as an accou-
cheur hates celibacy, because he gets nothing by it) is
employed to put in new sashes . . .

'I admit that nothing can be more reasonable than to
expect that a Catholic priest should starve to death, gen-
teelly and pleasantly, for the good of the Protestant religion; but is it equally reasonable to expect that he should
do so for the Protestant pews, and Protestant brick and
mortar? On an Irish Sabbath, the bell of a neat parish
church often summons to church only the parson and an oc-
casionally conforming clerk; while, two hundred yards off,
a thousand Catholics are huddled together in a miserable
hovel, and pelted by all the storms of heaven. Can anything
be more distressing than to see a venerable man pouring
forth sublime truths in tattered breeches, and depending
for his food upon the little offal he gets from his par-
ishioners? I venerate a human being who starves for his
principles, let them be what they may . . .'

Daniel O'Connell

In Ireland itself, one man dominated Irish politics during the
first half of the nineteenth century: Daniel O'Connell. He was
a Catholic, the son of a small landlord in County Kerry. He
was one of the first Catholics to take advantage of the limited
abolition of restrictions in the 1793 Act to become a barrister.
He rapidly became the most successful barrister in Ireland,
and then threw himself into political activity to such good effect that he would come to be known as 'the Liberator'; certainly, it was he more than anyone else who inspired the
identification of nationalism with Catholicism—or what
would later become the identification of 'Home Rule' with
'Rome Rule'.

He had two main political objectives. The one was Catholic emancipation, and the other was the repeal of the Union with Britain.

In 1823, O'Connell founded the Catholic Association, which aimed for the first time at a mass membership of *all* Catholics, both high and low, using the priests as local leaders and organisers. The subscription was only a penny a month— the 'Catholic rent', as it came to be called—which no one was too poor to afford. For the first time Catholic public opinion, Catholic muscle, was harnessed to a particular and specific end: to deliver a mass Catholic vote for parliamentary candidates in favour of Catholic emancipation.

O'Connell was a revolutionary, but he abhorred the thought of violence and bloodshed. But he was a magnificent agitator, and a hypnotic orator. According to the Irish popular writer, Canon D'Alton, writing in 1912:

'He had all the qualities that go to make a successful agitator. His frame was that of Hercules. He spoke Irish and English with equal fluency, and could therefore reach the masses of the people. It was on an Irish hillside, in the presence of an immense crowd, that he was at his best. His voice rang out as clearly as a bell, and as he spoke his audience laughed or wept, grew sad or gay, raised their heads high with pride when he told them they were the finest peasantry in the world, or muttered curses against the government when he recounted its evil deeds.'

The theme of O'Connell's oratory was stirring, irresistible, uplifting:

'The Catholic cause is on its majestic march; its progress is rapid and obvious. It is cheered in its advance and aided by all that is dignified and dispassionate. And its success is just as certain as the return of tomorrow's eve.'

Mass meetings, mass votes. The most spectacular triumph

came in 1828, when O'Connell himself stood in a parliamentary by-election for Clare. As a Catholic, O'Connell could not *sit* in Parliament, but there was nothing to stop him from *standing* for Parliament. On the day of the election, the local priests from all the county marshalled their regiments of voters to the polls. O'Connell's opponent, Vesey Fitzgerald, a well-liked, tolerant landowner who was himself sympathetic to Catholic Emancipation, did not have a chance. O'Connell was elected by a landslide.

The government was alarmed enough to capitulate. They knew that the next General Election would see another landslide; and in 1829, Parliament accordingly passed the Catholic Emancipation Act, removing all the remaining restrictions, and giving Catholics the right to become MPs, Cabinet ministers, judges and senior officers in the Army and Navy.

There is extant a remarkable document from this period— a Memorandum by Lord Anglesey, the Lord Lieutenant, of a conversation he had with 'the Liberator' on 29 July 1828, soon after O'Connell's victory in the Clare by-election. Anglesey had forewarned Sir Robert Peel, then Home Secretary, that O'Connell had requested an interview to discuss matters of law and order, the Catholic Association, emancipation, and so on. He told Peel, 'It will be my business to be very patient, very guarded, but not severely reserved, and whilst he is endeavouring to penetrate me, to try if I can make anything out of him.' It was indeed a far-ranging interview, but not in the least guarded; and the memorandum perhaps tells us more about Lord Anglesey than it does about Daniel O'Connell:

> 'Mr O'Connell ... with much mark of respect and peculiar calmness and mildness of manner expressed great regret at the unhappy state of the country which, he humbly suggested, was kept up by the frequent and unnecessary interference of the police and by the Protestants being generally armed.

An Irish peasant cabin in the 1770s from Arthur Young's *A Tour of Ireland.*

The Irish House of Commons 1790–1800. In the right hand front stand Harry Grattan and Henry Flood, both in the uniform of the Volunteers – the uniform which Grattan wore when he made his first speech against the union on 16th January 1800

Theobald Wolfe Tone.

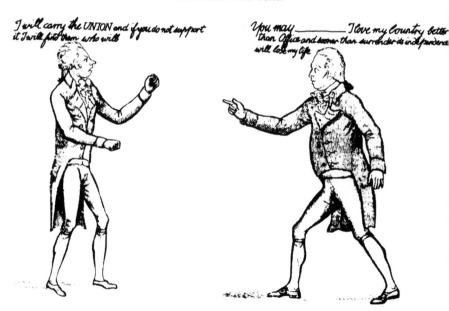

The British Prime Minister, William Pitt, threatening the Chancellor of the Irish Exchequer, Sir John Parnell, with loss of office if he does not support the Act of Union.

List of the 31 Towns, as they stand higher according to the produce of the Hearth Tax for the Year 1800 taken from Bod

1	Waterford	23	Mallow
2	Limerick	24	Athlone
✗ 3	Belfast	25	New Ross
4	Drogheda	✗ 26	Tralee
5	Newry	✗ 27	Cashell
6	Kilkenny	✗ 28	Dungannon
7	L. Derry	✗ 29	Portarlington
8	Galway	✗ 30	Enniskillen
✗ 9	Clonmell	✗ 31	Strabane
10	Wexford		
11	Youghall		
12	Bandon		
✗ 13	Armagh		
14	Dundalk		
15	Kinsale		
16	Lisburn		
✗ 17	Sligo		
✗ 18	Carlow		
✗ 19	Ennis		
20	Dungarvan		
21	Downpatrick		
✗ 22	Coleraine		

Those mark'd ✗ are Close

Lord Castlereagh's own list of the 31 boroughs selected, on the returns of the Hearth Tax, to send one MP to the Westminster Parliament after the 1800 Act of Union. By 'close' Castlereagh seems to have indicated those boroughs where the franchise lay with the Mayor and Corporation only. Altogether a hundred MPs went to Westminster from Ireland after the Act of Union.

Daniel O'Connell.

'He feared he might have been much misrepresented to me; that he was most anxious for the tranquillity of the country; that no effort should be wanting on his part to preserve it; that the Catholics were driven to the course they were now pursuing by the ungenerous treatment they had received; that they were sensible the progress they had made in their cause was solely attributable to the state of agitation and excitement that had been kept up; that they could now unhappily look to no other chance of success, and that it was therefore natural and to be expected that they should persevere in their course; that the object of the Association was to gain such an influence over the population as to secure the return to Parliament of men devoted to their cause and who, by constantly agitating the question and bringing it before the House of Commons, would drive ministers from their station or compel them to grant Emancipation . . .

'I proceeded to say that I deeply deplored the state of Ireland, in whose welfare I took a peculiar interest, etc, etc, etc. I differed with him respecting to the employment of the police, whose forbearance and moderation was generally the theme of praise; that they were frequently driven to the use of their arms to save their lives, and that in every instance the closest investigation of their conduct took place; that they were always amenable to the civil power; that the Protestants had, indeed, arms to a certain extent, but that they were prohibited from using them, and that the Catholics were under similar circumstances; that in point of fact no distinction existed as to regulation on that head.

'I gave him full credit for desiring tranquillity and being willing to use his efforts to preserve it, but I observed, when a very sensitive and half barbarous people were brought into great excitement, no one ought to presume that he had the power of controlling them.

'I admitted my belief that perseverance and agitation had gained for the Catholics the ground upon which they

stood; that no one was more anxious than myself for the
success of their cause— not even *he* whose language and
conduct had indeed often led me to doubt if he was sincere;
that so far from discouraging the agitation of the question,
the presenting of petitions, its frequent discussion, I would
advise a continuance in the same course, that the cause
should be advocated by the ablest members of both Houses
of Parliament; that I did not even object to the meeting of
the Association for the furtherance of their objects by every
fair *legal* means (*without quibble*); yet I could not but think
it might be well worth trying the experiment of discon-
tinuing them for a time, in the hope that such a proof of forbearance and acquiescence in the wishes of many of the
warmest friends of the Catholics, might produce a very ad-
vantageous effect. I expressed my doubt of the justness of
his expectations from the manner in which he hoped that
Ireland would be represented; that if it were attempted to
carry on future elections in the spirit of that of Clare, he
might depend upon a great reaction in England; that it
would become a "no popery" question, and that many of
the present supporters of the Catholics would lose their
seats in England.

'Mr O'Connell seemed extremely anxious to impress
upon my mind his abhorrence of insurrection and his conviction that none was to be expected. I assured him that I
had no apprehensions; that I could not bring my mind to
believe persons could be found hardy enough to attempt to
resist the law and break the peace; yet that I felt bound to be
prepared—that I was in fact prepared; and that happen
what might, I felt perfectly confident of being able to put
down insurrection in an instant. I spoke of my determination to act upon all occasions with the greatest forbearance . . . but that I could not shut my eyes to the possibility
of the most appalling of all cases—that of my being compelled, in aid of the King's troops, to arm the Orange population. What, said I, must be the dreadful consequences of

74

such a measure—war to extermination and the total extinc-
tion of all hope to the Catholics! For how could any government which had called for the energy of Protestants to put
down Catholic rebellion, ever propose to the former to receive into the Constitution upon an equality of rights, those
whom they had been called upon to assist in subduing from
open rebellion?

'This appeared to strike Mr O'Connell very forcibly. He
quite acquiesced in the observation, and said, not only
would such an event put off to an immeasurable term the
adjustment of the question, but in the event of insurrection
(which he again assured me was not to be apprehended)
even the power I possessed (and he thought it great) would
not enable me to suppress the rising of the Orangemen . . .

'I have omitted to state that, previously to entering into
conversation I desired Mr O'Connell to understand that
whatever I said or should thereafter say, was purely upon
my own account; that I had no authority to discuss, much
less to negotiate upon, the subject of Emancipation; that
negotiation in fact was inadmissable; and that whenever
anything should be done, it must be done by the legislature without treaty, although of course communications
of a private character might pass between individuals in-
terested . . .

'O'Connell is the vainest of men and the easiest taken
by a good bait . . . My firm belief is that O'Connell is perfectly sincere. I should be laughed at for my gullibility,
but I repeat that I believe him sincere; that he has a good
heart and means well and means indeed always what he
says; but that he is volatile and unsteady and so vain that
he cannot resist momentary applause.'

For the next twelve years after emancipation, O'Connell,
now a Member of Parliament, played a quiet political game,
supporting the English Whig Party, once he had reached an
understanding with it in 1834. But Ireland itself was by no

means liberated, and when the Tories returned to power under Sir Robert Peel, O'Connell launched his second great agitation in 1841—the campaign for the repeal of the Union. His tactics would be the same—monster mass meetings to organise Catholic opinion, and no violence.

Nothing like these mass meetings had ever been seen in Ireland before—like the meeting of hundreds of thousands that gathered at the historic site of Tara in 1843, as described in the reminiscences of an eye-witness, Charles Gavan Duffy, in *Young Ireland* (1880):

'. . . it was estimated that the number in attendance on O'Connell [from Dublin] did not fall short of ten thousand. Before the procession had arrived within a dozen miles of the historic hill large crowds were discovered who had come from distant places during the night . . . Each town was preceded by its band in the national uniforms of green and white, and by banners with suitable inscriptions. They were mustered by mounted marshals, distinguished by badges, horsemen four deep, footmen six deep, and the men of each parish marched, O'Connell afterwards declared, "as if they were in battalions". Three miles from the hill the vehicles had to be abandoned; from the immensity of the attendance there was space only for footmen . . . Around the base of the hill the bands and banners were mustered. The bands amounted to forty, an equipment sufficient for an army; the banners were past counting.

'The procession however was but as a river discharging itself into an ocean. The whole district was covered with men. The population within a day's march began to arrive on foot shortly after daybreak, and continued to arrive, on all sides, and by every available approach, till noon. It was impossible from any one point to see the entire meeting; the hill rose almost perpendicular out of the level plain, and hill and plain were covered with a multitude "countless as the bearded grain". The number is supposed to have reached between 500,000 and 750,000 persons. It was ordinarily spoken of as a million, and was certainly a muster of men such as had never before assembled in one place in Ireland, in peace or war.'

The tide of public support must have seemed irresistible. But O'Connell was up against sterner opposition this time. Sir Robert Peel, who had reluctantly agreed to grant Emancipation, would have no truck whatsoever with repeal of the Union:

'There is no influence, no power, no authority which the prerogatives of the crown and the existing law give to the government, which shall not be exercised for the purpose of maintaining the Union; the dissolution of which would involve not merely the repeal of an Act of Parliament, but the dismemberment of this great empire . . . Deprecating as I do all war, but above all, civil war, yet there is no alternative which I do not think preferable to the dismemberment of this empire.'

There followed a spectacular exercise in brinkmanship. O'Connell had scheduled the last and biggest of his mass meetings for the equally historic site of Clontarf, on the outskirts of Dublin, where the Irish hero, Brian Boru, had died in the hour of a famous victory over the Vikings. For this meeting the government poured in extra troops. Naval warships lurked menacingly in Dublin Bay. The guns of Dublin Fort were trained on the meeting place. And a few hours before the meeting was due to start, the government banned it.

O'Connell was in a dilemma. He had always argued against armed insurrection: but he was also convinced that any government would yield to peaceful organised mass opinion, as they had yielded over Catholic Emancipation. Now Peel was challenging his principles and his integrity; and O'Connell, to the secret dismay of many, no doubt, stood by his deepest principles and cancelled the meeting.

Along with other leaders of the Repeal Movement, O'Connell was later imprisoned for a year. When he emerged, he was a spent political force. He had aroused the political consciousness of the Catholic masses, only to lose everything when the chips were down. But perhaps a more serious effect of his agitation was that it served to make nationalism an exclusively Catholic preoccupation. The more that O'Connell mobilised the Catholics, the less there seemed to be in it for the Protestants. It was not unlike the story of Gandhi, whose Hindu emphasis increasingly alienated the Moslems in India and led first to partition and then to an inevitable bloodbath after his death.

There was one other outcome of the O'Connell agitations that would cast a long shadow; from it emerged a group of fiery young politicians whose movement was known as Young Ireland. They came to despise O'Connell for his pacifism and, worse, they believed him to have lost his nerve. *They* would never shrink from violence:

> 'War—the exposure of ourselves to wounds, toil and death—is as much our duty in a just cause as any other mode of sustaining justice . . .
>
> 'We feel no wish to encourage the occasion of war, but whenever the occasion comes, may bold hearts and strong arms be found to plan, lead and fight.'

The thinking of the Young Ireland movement was to become the Bible of later generations of fanatical idealists preaching fiery revolution, although the movement itself would fizzle out in quarrels and an ill-planned insurrection in 1848 that failed completely. But before that abortive rising, Ireland was to be hit by one of the most terrible natural disasters any country could suffer: the great Potato Famine of the 1840s.

PART III

A Nation's Wealth is in her Land: 1845-1891

I mentioned earlier that I had been greeted in Dublin by a Guinness advertisement inviting all and sundry to 'take up Irish History tonight'. But, of course, Guinness isn't the only Irish history you'll find in an Irish bar. As the night wears on and the singing gets under way, so the sad, sad story of martyrs dead and causes lost wells up, and the 1798 Rebellion is as yesterday. The tunes may change as the night wears on, but the theme remains the same: the combined celebration and mourning of the heroes who fought for Ireland's freedom while her suffering people groaned under the yoke of English oppression, all blood and glory and the sweet pain of sacrifice. If you are in an Ulster bar, of course, it could well be 'The sash my father wore' that you would hear. How keenly it all reminds one of G. K. Chesterton's striking stanza from the *Ballad of the White Horse*:

> For the great Gaels of Ireland
> Are the men that God made mad,
> For all their wars are merry,
> And all their songs are sad.

Balladry and poetry are essential ingredients in the fabric of Irish society; indeed, you still meet Irishmen who, after recounting a long and eccentric incident that took place in their village twenty years ago, will end up quite naturally by saying, 'Of course, they made a song about it.' The ballads that commemorate the legendary deeds, the heroic stands, the battles against impossible odds—these enshrine the received version of history which bypasses school and textbook, and remains largely impervious to academic correction. Modern Irish historians may work at their Historiographical Revolution and spread from universities to schools a more objective and dispassionate view of Irish history, but the ballads continue to be sung, and to be taught to the next generation; and certainly, whether you talk to the historians or listen to the bar-ballads, it is hard to avoid the impression that Ireland has had more than her share of misfortune down the centuries: it has been one fearsome crisis after another, it seems.

In America the song 'Brother, can you spare a dime?' is an instant reminder of the misery of the 1930s Depression when millions went hungry—and we accept it as such; so surely nothing deserves an elegy more than the terrible catastrophe which befell Ireland in the middle of the nineteenth century when the 'praties', or potatoes, failed and a million people actually died of starvation. The following verses may be as ersatz as Bing Crosby's evocation of hunger pangs: but if ever a song had a right to be sad, this famine song is it.

> Oh, the praties they grow small
>   over here, over here,
> Oh, the praties they grow small
>   and we dig them in the fall
> And we eat them skins and all
>   over here, over here.
>
> Oh, I wish that we were geese
>   night and morn, night and morn,
> Oh, I wish that we were geese
>   for they fly and take their ease
> And live and die in peace
>   eating corn, eating corn.
>
> Oh, we're trampled in the dust
>   over here, over here,

Yes, we're trampled in the dust
   but the Lord in whom we trust
Will give us crumb for crust
   over here, over here.

The Great Famine

The story of the second half of the nineteenth century in Ireland is dominated by two major themes, two protracted struggles that were closely interlinked: ownership of the land, and the campaign for Home Rule. But what overshadowed the beginning of the period was the Great Potato Famine. The famine was the most dreadful natural disaster to strike any part of the British Isles since the Black Death devastated England in the fourteenth century. In four years of horror and human suffering, from 1845 to 1848, Ireland lost a quarter of her population, and eye-witness scenes of the appalling privations of the people are burned deep into the folk memory of the Irish. This is how Nicholas Cummins, a well-known magistrate of Cork, described the horrifying conditions he found in the village of Skibbereen, in a letter he sent to the Duke of Wellington and also to *The Times* in December 1846:

'Without apology or preface, I presume so far to trespass on your Grace as to state to you, and by the use of your illustrious name, to present to the British public the following statement of what I have myself seen within the last three days. Having for many years been intimately connected with the western portion of the County of Cork, and possessing some small property there, I thought it right personally to investigate the truth of several lamentable accounts which had reached me of the appalling state of misery to which that part of the country was reduced. I accordingly went on the 15th instant to Skibbereen, and to give the instance of one townland which I visited, as an example of the state of the entire coast district, I shall state simply what I there saw.

'Being aware that I should have to witness scenes of frightful hunger, I provided myself with as much bread as five men could carry, and on reaching the spot I was surprised to find the wretched hamlet apparently deserted. I entered some of the hovels to ascertain the cause, and the scenes which presented themselves were such as no tongue or pen can convey the slightest idea of. In the first, six famished and ghastly skeletons, to all appearances dead, were huddled in a corner on some filthy straw, their sole covering what seemed a ragged horsecloth, their wretched legs hanging about, naked above the knees. I approached with horror, and found by a low moaning they were alive— they were in fever, four children, a woman and what had once been a man. It is impossible to go through the detail. Suffice to say, that in a few minutes I was surrounded by at least 200 such phantoms, such frightful spectres as no words can describe, either from famine or from fever. Their demoniac yells are still ringing in my ears, and their horrible images are fixed upon my brain. My heart sickens at the recital, but I must go on.

'In another case, decency would forbid what follows, but it must be told. My clothes were nearly torn off in my endeavour to escape from the throng of pestilence around, when my neckcloth was seized from behind by a grip which compelled me to turn. I found myself grasped by a woman with an infant just born in her arms and the remains of a filthy sack across her loins—the sole covering of herself and baby. The same morning the police opened a house on the adjoining lands, which was observed shut for many days, and two frozen corpses were found, lying upon the mud floor, half devoured by rats.

'A mother, herself in a fever, was seen the same day to drag out the corpse of her child, a girl about twelve, perfectly naked, and leave it half covered with stones. In another house within 500 yards of the cavalry station at Skibbereen, the dispensary doctor found seven wretches lying unable to move, under the same cloak. One had been dead many hours, but the others were unable to move either themselves or the corpse.'

How could such scenes have happened? Indeed, how could they have been allowed to happen? How, in a civilised West European country, could a million people starve to death little more than a century ago—a country, remember, that was then in full union with England and had been part and parcel of the United Kingdom since the union of the parliaments in 1800? One bitter answer that many Irish have always believed is that it happened because the English wanted it to happen. It makes a cynical scenario. Ireland was becoming grossly over-populated at the time, causing massive poverty and unemployment. When the potato blight struck, it wiped out the only source of food available to the peasants—and the English authorities were quite content to let the ensuing Famine solve the population problem at a stroke, by withholding aid or relief. It was, according to this Irish view, a devious form of genocide: genocide by omission, as it were, as blatant as when the Russian Army stood back and allowed the Polish Underground forces in Warsaw to be slaughtered by the retreating Germans in 1944.

This highly emotive version is now recognised by all serious historians as a gross distortion of the reality. The Famine, in fact, was the outcome of economic forces that had been building up for a long time, not of deliberate political policies. With hindsight, we can now see that a problem over land had been growing steadily for decades. The population of Ireland was soaring: from five million in 1800, to six and a half million in 1821, to more than eight million in 1841. There simply was not enough land to feed everybody. Another factor was the Napoleonic War, which drove up the world price of grain; until then, Irish agriculture had been essentially pastoral, but now more and more grassland was broken up to grow corn. To obtain the extra labour required, the landlord or tenant farmer would lease a little piece of ground to a peasant, who would pay the rent with his labour. Here he would build a mud cabin; and to feed himself and his family, he would grow potatoes.

The potato was ideal for the circumstances. It was nutritious and healthy, especially if supplemented with milk—a complete food in itself, rich in protein. A small patch of ground could give an excellent yield. More and more, the Irish peasantry came to be totally reliant on the potato as their staple diet, and each plot of land became subdivided into smaller and smaller units to enable sons to marry young and start families of their own. A vicious circle was developing, practically unnoticed—until the blight struck.

The *Gardeners' Chronicle* of 13 September 1845 carried an ominous announcement:

> 'We stop the press with very great regret to announce that the potato murrain has unequivocally declared itself in Ireland. The crops about Dublin are suddenly perishing.'

The potato blight, or murrain, had ravaged the eastern seaboard of North America three years earlier. Then, during a long spell of wet weather in July 1845, it crossed the Atlantic and attacked the potato crop in southern England. By September it had reached Ireland. It spread like wildfire until it affected about half of the whole country. Over huge areas the promising potato crop now lay black and rotting in the fields.

The government reacted promptly. Sir Robert Peel, the Prime Minister, appointed a scientific commission to investigate the new disease, but the experts failed to discover that it was a fungus growth and not a disease of the potato itself; so the 70,000 pamphlets printed by the commission with instructions on how to save the crops were wasted—and, anyway, the peasants couldn't read them. But Peel also launched an immediate relief programme. He arranged the purchase of

£100,000 worth of Indian corn, or maize, from America; he set up local Relief Committees with government grants, and fostered public works for the unemployed, with the government paying half the costs, so that the peasants would have some money with which to buy the American maize.

In the nineteenth-century context of free enterprise and non-intervention, Peel's moves were humane. But one aspect of them has damned him for ever in Irish eyes—the fact that he insisted that Irish grain should continue to be exported. Grain was the staple of the Irish economy. Tenants paid their rent with it, landlords paid their running costs with it. To have interfered with the export of grain would have stultified the whole economy. Peel was also worried that world prices for grain would rise because of the sudden change in supply and demand, and that is why he bought maize secretly in America and insisted that Irish grain should continue to be exported. And in order to protect the farmers and businessmen who made a living from grain, he insisted that the Irish peasants should *pay* for the relief supplies of maize wherever possible. Soaring prices in Ireland would have made conditions even worse, he reasoned, and dumping free maize would have destroyed the business economy. Indeed, world grain prices were already so high that there was a grave risk that any further increase would bring famine to England, too, where the staple diet was bread. Everyone was afraid that whatever was done would only make matters worse. Nineteenth-century politics had no answer to a problem on this scale—and the famines in Bangladesh and elsewhere show that the twentieth century is not very good at dealing with it, either.

Under the circumstances, Peel probably had no choice; but he has been consistently reviled for his actions, even though he committed political suicide as a leader of the Tory Party by advocating the repeal of the Corn Laws in an attempt to achieve cheap corn for Ireland.

In 1846 the potato crop failed again, and this time, the

failure was complete. The rector of the Church of Ireland parish of Ballynascreen, County Londonderry, the Reverend Samuel Montgomery, noted in his register:

> 'On the three last days of July and the first six days of August 1846 the potatoes were suddenly attacked, when in their full growth, with a sudden blight. The tops were first observed to wither and then, on looking to the roots, the tubers were found hastening to decomposition. The entire crop that in the month of July appeared so luxuriant, about the 15th of August manifested only blackened and withered stems.
>
> 'The whole atmosphere in the month of September was tainted with the odour of the decaying potatoes, i.e. the tubers.'

A new Whig government under Lord John Russell, wedded to its philosophy of *laissez-faire* economic principles, decreed that there should be no more government buying of food, and that supplies should be left to private enterprise. Food prices soared as a result, and mass starvation loomed that winter. One landowner in County Londonderry, the Rt. Hon. George Dawson, Sir Robert Peel's brother-in-law, wrote to the Chairman of the Board of Customs in London, Sir Thomas Fremantle, to describe the distress in South Derry in the winter of 1846–7:

> 'I really have not had heart to write to you before, for I had nothing to communicate except the heart rending scenes of misery which I daily witness. I wish I had never come here. If I had known what I was to encounter in this hitherto happy district, I should have spared myself the pain of witnessing a misery which, with every feeling of compassion and every expenditure within my means, I can do no more than most inadequately and feebly relieve.
>
> 'I can think of nothing else than the wretched condition of this wretched people. We are comparatively well off in

this neighbourhood. There is no want of food; but it is at such a price, as to make it totally impossible for a poor man to support his family with the wages he receives. I do not exaggerate when I tell you that from the moment I open my hall door in the morning until dark, I have a crowd of women and children crying out for something to save them from starving. The men, except the old and infirm, stay away and show the greatest patience and resignation. I have been obliged to turn my kitchen into a bakery and soup shop to enable me to feed the miserable children and mothers that cannot be sent away empty. So great is their distress that they actually faint on getting food into their stomachs. The only reply to my question of "What do you want?" is, "I want something to eat," is so simple, so universal, that it tells its own tale, and neither rags nor sickness nor worn out faces or emaciated limbs can make their situation more truly pitiable than these few words. The gentry, the shopkeepers, the clergy are making every effort in their power to relieve the people by subscriptions and incessant attention, but what can be done when thousands are daily applying for one meal a day? . . . If provisions were cheaper, we might look forward with hope, but if no reduction in the price of food shall take place, hundreds will die of starvation.'

As the full horror of the calamity became apparent, the government was forced to take further action. It initiated a further programme of public works to create more employment. Yet what help it offered was so hedged about with bureaucratic rules and regulations as to lose much of its effectiveness and give the impression of callous heartlessness. The local Relief Committees that had been formed spontaneously in their hundreds all over Ireland were sent the following circular from the Commissariat Relief Office in Dublin in December 1846, to prevent the abuse of public money for public works:

'To admit all applicants would be productive of ruinous consequences, and is not necessary, as many persons who apply are known to have other resources. A scrutiny is, therefore, indispensable to keep down the amount of Local Taxation which the Works will occasion—as well as to distribute the employment among the really necessitous classes.

'*Applicants who have not any Land* should not be admitted on the registry, for employment, until it is clearly ascertained that they cannot get work in their usual pursuits; that they have been for some time unemployed; and have no other present source of maintenance.

'*Applicants who have Land* should not be registered, unless the Committee shall be satisifed that every person admitted is actually destitute of means of subsistence, and cannot obtain them otherwise than by employment on the Public Works.

'*The extent of Land* held by each Applicant should be carefully ascertained; and although there are cases in which holders of a larger quantity than has been ordinarily held for Potato Crop, may be rendered destitute by some combination of unfortunate circumstances, still it is considered, that the occupation of more Land than may have been used for producing the yearly supply of Potatoes, must be held by the Committee as disqualifying the applicants from employment without satisfactory evidence of destitution, as well as proof of inability to procure subsistence, unless employed on the Public Works.

'It is considered that any person whose land may be valued on the Rate Books at £6 or upwards, is likely to possess means of providing for the maintenance of his family without resorting to the Relief Works; and the application of every such person should therefore be rejected at once, unless the most undoubted evidence of destitution shall be presented.

'In fixing on "£6 or upwards" as an amount of value requiring rejection of the applicant, it is not intended that lower amounts should be regarded as entitling the occupiers of such lesser holdings to admission without questioning the necessity for relief in each case. In every case the most rigid scrutiny is necessary for public protection, and the Committee cannot shrink from the duty of making it.

'The evidence of destitution which the Committee should require is not intended to be ordinary viva voce testimony, but searching local investigation, made in Committee, as well as in the Townlands.'

The government's policy had been to try to push the burden of relief on to the Irish Board of Works and the Irish landlords; and despite the mythology of callous evictions and brutal indifference, there is ample evidence that many landlords did what they could, by reducing rents or by providing work or food. One of the greatest and most enlightened landlords in Ireland, the Marquess of Waterford, who owned some 75,000 acres in Counties Waterford, Wicklow, and Londonderry, wrote to his kinsman and agent, John Beresford, on Christmas Day, 1846:

'I have received your letter stating that you think £300 would be sufficient to give assistance to the poor on my property. I have established soup kitchens in this county and find them very beneficial. I wish you to set them up in the different parishes in which I have property . . .

'I conceive that many in each parish will subscribe, but my great object is to support the destitute on my estate. I have given the amount to each parish according to the number of acres, but if you can improve the distribution let me know. You can commence the weekly subscription from Monday next, and set the pot a-boiling as soon as you can. The position ought to be the most central. In some places a trifle is charged per quart, which makes it go further, but you can do as you think best. I am sure the clergy will be willing to assist in these works.'

Things would have been even worse without the huge sums of money raised through private charity. The Quakers and many other agencies in England and America gave generously. As it was, the suffering was unimaginable. As starving mobs poured into the towns, typhus and relapsing fever raged, bacillary dysentery reached epidemic proportions. The *Thirteenth Annual Report* of the Poor Law Commissioners in 1847 contains some terrible statistics; for instance, in the paupers' workhouse run by the Lurgan Poor Law Guardians, the number of deaths rose sharply week by week throughout January 1847—18 in the first week, 36 in the second, 55 in the third, 58 in the fourth, and 68 in the week following. The Medical Officer, Dr Bell, explained the increase in a report to the Commissioners:

'From the scarcity and consequent high prices of provisions, and the great dislike of going to the workhouse among the lower classes here, many diseases are now prevalent in the country, and the great majority of new admissions are, when brought into the house, at the point of death, in a moribund state. Many have been known to die on the road, and others on being raised from their beds to come to the workhouse have died before they could be put into the cart, and numbers have died in less than 24 hours subsequent to their admission. Therefore mortality in the workhouse is much greater than under ordinary circumstances, and it is a well-known fact that many dying persons are sent for admission merely that coffins may be obtained for them at the expense of the Union . . .'

One could write endlessly about the horrors of the Famine. But there are three main points that I think need to be stressed.

The first is that modern historians, who have been concentrating more and more on individual counties and parishes, are beginning to show that the effects of the Famine were neither uniform nor nationwide. They were selective. The Famine had the worst impact where there was rural over-population and excessive sub-division of land. The towns-people did much better, as did the larger tenant farmers who went in for grain, and the much better organised agricultural communities in Ulster, where tenants had long been allowed to benefit from any improvements they made on the land they leased. The Famine was essentially a peasant scourge—and a Catholic peasant scourge at that; so further fuel was added to the age-old sectarian resentments of a people who felt them-selves oppressed under a Protestant Ascendancy.

In the second place, the Famine did substantially improve conditions in Ireland, for those who survived it. The dramatic fall in the population brought it roughly into balance with available resources. Farms could be enlarged into more viable units, and agriculture in Ireland forged ahead very success-fully for the next thirty years. This aftermath only hardened suspicions that the Famine had been allowed to happen, or even artificially induced, in order to achieve that very end.

Thirdly, and most important perhaps, was the mass emi-gration that took place. A million people or so fled the country, mostly to North America, and they took with them a legacy of hatred that has lasted to this day. The bitterest went to the USA, while many others remained under the British flag in Canada. The emigrant survivors of the Famine in ef-fect exported the 'Irish problem' to America.

The American Connection

Emigration from the stricken island became almost a panic—anything to get away from the shadow of death. But to emi-grate was not necessarily to escape; many of the emigrant ships came to be known as 'coffin ships'. Stephen de Vere, member of a well-known family in County Limerick, deliber-ately took steerage passage on one such vessel to Quebec in order 'that he might speak as a witness respecting the sufferings of emigrants':

> 'Before the emigrant has been a week at sea he is an altered man . . . How can it be otherwise? Hundreds of poor people, men, women and children, of all ages from the drivelling idiot of 90 to the babe just born, huddled together, without light, without air, wallowing in filth, and breathing a foetid atmosphere, sick in body, dispirited in heart . . . the fevered patients lying between the sound in sleeping places so narrow, as almost to deny them a change of position . . . by their agonised ravings disturbing those around them . . . living without food or medicine except as administered by the hand of casual charity, dying without spiritual consolation and buried without the rites of the church.'

The cost of a fare to Quebec for a man and wife with four children was £6 at the time. To New York, it was considerably higher—£21. Usually, ships only sailed in spring and summer, but in 1846–7, for the first time in history, emigration continued throughout the winter. Some 30,000 emigrants went to the USA that winter; throughout 1847, 85,000 people left from Irish ports. Many passages were assisted by landlords, with clothing and money for fares. But getting the fare paid was no guarantee of the future. In November 1847, a ship bringing tenants from Lord Palmerston's estate in Sligo arrived in New Brunswick in Canada. The passengers were almost in a state of nudity, and ninety-nine per cent of them became a public charge immediately. They were widows with helpless young families, decrepit old men, and women riddled with disease. The citizens of St John promptly declared that they could not cope, and posted notices in the streets offering a free passage back to Ireland!

In general, the mortality on the 'coffin ships' was appalling. An inscription on a monument in the cemetery in Grosse Island in Canada, one of the immigrant landing-places, needs no further exposition:

'In this secluded spot lie the mortal remains of 5,294 persons who, flying from pestilence and famine in Ireland in the year 1847, found in America but a grave.'

Those who survived the rigours of the voyage, and the hostility of some North American towns which felt overwhelmed by this decanting of destitute refugees into their midst, cherished in their hearts, and nurtured in the hearts of their descendants, a burning hatred of the English government which had so signally failed to deal with a catastrophe of the magnitude of the Famine. All the grief, the humiliation, the bitterness was concentrated against England, and would be constantly refuelled by later generations of immigrants. This hatred was now no longer confined within Ireland's borders; it ceased to be an internal United Kingdom problem, and became an international one—especially in America. A contemporary comment by the politician John Bright on the emigrations helps to explain why successive American administrations still try to take a hand in efforts to resolve the 'Irish problem':

'In whatever quarter of the world an Irishman sets his foot, there stands a bitter, an implacable enemy of England . . . There are hundreds of thousands—I suppose there are millions—of the population of the United States of America who are Irish by birth, or by immediate descent; and be it remembered, Irishmen settled in the United States have a large influence in public affairs. They sometimes sway the election of Members of the Legislature, and may even affect the election of the President of the Republic. There may come a time when questions of a critical nature will be agitated between the governments of Great Britain and the United States; and it is certain that at such a time the Irish in that country will throw their whole weight into the scale against this country . . .'

93

No doubt the deep resentment was sharpened by the knowledge that many of those who had not been forced to emigrate from Ireland were doing well. The dealers and middlemen, like middlemen everywhere, profited from the Famine. Many landlords were bankrupted by the sudden loss of rents and the help they had given their starving people; but the tenant farmer with a good-sized holding and mixed production hardly suffered at all. Indeed, Irish agriculture as a whole lost nothing by the virtual liquidation of the destitute peasant class. But rationalisations of this kind do nothing to assuage the unforgotten sorrows of the time, any more than they do for the memories of the Highland Clearances in Scotland—quite the opposite, in fact.

In the aftermath of the Famine came the Industrial Revolution—especially in Ulster. The linen industry flourished for a time, to be followed by an even more prosperous cotton industry in the 1870s. The city of Belfast burgeoned, and its population soon topped the 100,000 mark. In 1853 a shipyard was started there which soon, as Harland and Wolff, would become the largest shipyard in the world. Heavy industry flourished. In fact, some Irish historians now suggest that the Industrial Revolution, favouring as it did Ulster more than any other area in Ireland, is much more significant in history than the original Ulster Plantation in the early seventeenth century. It brought another influx of skilled workers into Ulster, Protestant workers, many of them from Scotland, while unskilled Catholic workers were relegated to second-class work and second-class areas. The Industrial Revolution increased the prosperity of Ulster in relation to the rest of Ireland, and thereby helped to foment even further the political discontent in the south; but it also served to tie Ulster sentiment and Ulster trade ever more closely with industrial Britain.

The Fenians

In the years following the Great Famine the spirit of resistance to British rule was at its lowest ebb in Ireland. But in North America it burned brightly; and ten years later, in 1858, it found overt expression in the foundation of a revolutionary movement called the Irish Republican Brotherhood. It was founded simultaneously in Dublin and New York, and it was an Irish-American leader who suggested that the members of the movement should call themselves 'Fenians'—the name given to the legendary warriors of ancient Ireland. Not for the first time, Irish patriots were seeking inspiration and justification from the mists, or myths, of history.

In their case it must have seemed appropriate, for they believed that Britain would never concede independence except to physical force. Constitutional agitation had been tried, by Daniel O'Connell and his followers, and had ultimately failed. The Fenians believed that the only effective resort was to violence. To that end, they set up a secret, armed organisation which would be ready to strike when the time was ripe, and every member had to take a secret, conspiratorial oath:

> 'I, in the presence of Almighty God, do solemnly swear allegiance to the Irish Republic and I will do my very utmost, while life lasts, to defend its independence and integrity; I will yield implicit obedience in all things, not contrary to the laws of God, to the commands of my superior officers. So help me God.'

The American Irish played an immensely important part in the movement, because it so happened that they had been given a unique opportunity of learning military techniques by hard experience in the American Civil War which broke out in 1861. There were Irish regiments in both the Northern and the Southern armies. When the Civil War ended in 1865, there was a trained cadre of Irish-born officers ready and eager to take up civil war again, even in Ireland.

A Fenian rising in Ireland was scheduled for 1865, when relations between Britain and America were strained. But the American Fenians could not agree amongst themselves. In Ireland thousands of men enrolled as Fenians and prepared for action; but the looked-for Americans failed to arrive. It was not until 1867 that a Fenian-manned ship sailed from Boston and managed to land some men and arms in Ireland. But the rising was disorganised and doomed from the start, and the British government forces had little difficulty in quelling it.

The failure of the Fenian uprising in 1867 seemed complete. The Irish Republican Brotherhood only just survived, not so much as a movement but as a lingering sentiment. But at least the 1867 rebellion had one direct effect. Almost for the first time, the battle for Irish independence was carried to England, and now the English experienced Fenian violence in the streets of their own cities. A Fenian group attempted to raid the arsenal of Chester Castle but were foiled. When the two leading Fenians were arrested, a rescue attempt was launched as they were being driven through Manchester in a prison van. A crowd of sympathisers managed to blow open the doors of the van and get the prisoners out; but in the course of the exploit, a policeman was accidentally shot dead. Five men were arrested and tried, and three of them were found guilty on what was widely condemned as very dubious evidence; they were subsequently hanged for murder, in what turned out to be one of the last public hangings in Britain. In this way, Irish mythology gained a new batch of dead heroes—the Manchester Martyrs—while the spread of Fenian violence to the streets of England had a profound and lasting effect on public opinion there.

Two related and highly significant political attitudes emerged from the outburst. In England, the Liberal leader, William Gladstone, was so deeply affected by this violent demonstration of Irish nationalism that he embarked on a programme of what he called 'justice for Ireland'. And in Ireland, after the failure of the Fenian revolt, the nationalist impetus shifted towards constitutional means.

For his part, Gladstone used his first administration in 1868 to disestablish the episcopalian Church of Ireland, thus undermining the privileged position of the Protestant Ascendancy: he also tried to promote Bills to protect Irish tenants from arbitrary eviction, and to create universities for Catholics. These proposals did not succeed immediately, but they laid the groundwork for later achievements.

The Birth of the Home Rule Movement

Meanwhile, in Ireland, a leading Irish MP called Isaac Butt in 1870 founded a new Home Rule movement, the Home Government Association, whose objective was to achieve by constitutional means a limited form of parliamentary Home Rule without resort to revolutionary violence:

> 'To obtain for our country the right and privilege of managing our own affairs by a Parliament assembled in Ireland, composed of Her Majesty, the Sovereign, and her successors, and the Lords and Commons of Ireland. To secure for that Parliament the right of legislating for and regarding all matters relating to the internal affairs of Ireland.'

In the aftermath of the Fenian failure, this was a striking reversion to moderation and conservatism: to a policy of devolution rather than revolution. To that end, Isaac Butt worked patiently and conscientiously to persuade the House of Commons to consider Ireland's claims for separate nationhood. But it was not until a new personality emerged to lead the Home Rule party that the House of Commons began perforce to take those claims seriously. That leader was Charles Stewart Parnell.

Charles Stewart Parnell

Parnell is one of the most charismatic figures in Ireland's political history. When he was elected to Parliament as a Home Ruler in 1875 he was only twenty-nine years old. He was handsome and wealthy, a Protestant landowner who was very much a part of high society, an anglicised Irishman who was none the less passionately devoted to the cause of Irish nationalism. His mother was a daughter of Admiral Charles Stewart, whose name her son bore: Parnell's very identity enshrined a hero of the British-American War of 1812 whose heritage was not of defeat by the British but victory against them.

Parnell soon found himself in disagreement with Isaac Butt's gentlemanly approach to the House of Commons. In one of his speeches Butt had said:

> 'I took the liberty some time ago at Limerick to lay down what I believed was the policy to pursue, and that was to make an assault all along the whole line of English misgovernment, and to bring forward every grievance of Ireland, and to press the English House of Commons for their redress; and I believed, and believe it still, that if once we got liberal-minded Englishmen fairly to consider how they would redress the grievance of Irish misgovernment, they would come in the end to the conclusion that they had but one way of giving us good government, and that was by allowing us to govern ourselves.'

Parnell's response was typical:

> 'Mr Butt has very fairly explained the policy that he has carried out during the three or four years that this Parliament has lasted . . . Now I gladly agree with Mr Butt that it is very possible, and very probable, that he would be able to persuade a fair-minded Englishman in the direction that he has indicated; but still I do not think that the House

of Commons is mainly composed of fair-minded Englishmen. If we had to deal with men who were capable of listen-
ing to fair arguments there would be every hope of success
for the policy of Mr Butt as carried out in past sessions; but
we are dealing with political parties who really consider the
interests of their political organisations as paramount,
beyond every other consideration.'

Parnell's tactic in the House of Commons was to make an
unmitigated nuisance of himself, using all the wiles of debat-
ing, questioning and amendment to obstruct the business of
the House until Parliament was obliged to pay attention to the
Irish question. He was ultimately so successful that ten years
after his election he could control eighty-five Irish Members of
Parliament who often held the balance of power between successive Liberal and Conservative administrations.

But that would come later. It was Parnell's tactics of solo
obstructionism that first won him the attention of the Fenians
in America, as organised in the movement *Clan na Gael*,
whose dominant personality was John Devoy. *Devoy's Post
Bag, 1871–1928*, and his own *Recollections of an Irish Rebel*,
give a clear indication of how the American Fenians began to
cultivate Parnell. A letter from James O'Kelly to Devoy, dated
5 August 1877, is highly illuminating:

'I had a long chat with Parnell and Biggar, the former is
a man of promise, I think he ought *to be supported*. He has
the idea I held at the starting of the Home Rule organisation—that is the creation of a political link between the
conservative and radical nationalists. I suppose the lunatics
will be content with nothing less than the moon—and *they*
will never get it. The effect of Parnell's attitude has been
simply tremendous and if he were supported by twenty or
thirty instead of seven he could render really important services. He has many of the qualities of leadership—and time
will give him more. He is cool—extremely so and resolute.
With the right kind of support behind him and a band of

99

real nationalists in the House of Commons he would so remould Irish public opinion as to clear away many of the stumbling blocks in the way of progressive action.'

In America, Devoy was setting the political course for the Fenians in resolutions like these:

'1   That we deem the present a fitting opportunity to proclaim our conviction of Ireland's right to an independent national existence. That as Ireland has never forfeited her right to independence, and as no action on the part of England has given any justification for the acceptance of the Union, we hereby protest against all attempts at compromise, and renew our resolve to work for the complete overthrow of British domination.

'2   That the landlord system forced on the Irish people by English legislation is a disgrace to humanity and to the civilisation of the present century. It is the direct cause of the expatriation of millions of the Irish race, and of the miserable condition of the Irish peasantry. That as the land of Ireland belongs to the people of Ireland, the abolition of the foreign landlord system and the substitution of one by which the tiller of the soil will be fixed permanently upon it, and holding directly of the State, is the only true solution of the Irish land question, which an Irish Republic can alone effect.'

Meanwhile, the American Fenians were still busy raising money for arms for the nationalists in Ireland. A coded letter dated 23 April 1879 is an indication of their continuing activity:

'It is now about ten months since 17,000 dollars was sent to Pascalville [Paris] to supply agricultural implements [arms] to labourers in country around Port Osborne [Ireland]. So far as we can learn not one has gone into that country. Now, as Mr Clinch [Carroll] called for 25,000 dollars from stockholders soon after for the same purpose, he

finds himself within three months of time of annual settlement 1st August, and *not one hoe* or the like in the hands of
those who are to use them (if anybody ever does in that
field), and so far as he [Clinch] can learn, not a squad yet
prepared for their proper use.'

Parnell, in whom the Fenians saw a way of marrying the
revolutionary and devolutionary wings of the nationalist
movement, was invited to America in 1880, and in speeches at
Cleveland and Cincinnati, in January and February of that
year, he astutely accepted the support of the Fenians without
fully committing himself to their organisation.

The 'Land War', 1879–82

The coming together of the twin thrusts of Irish nationalism,
Home Rule and land reform, was dramatically assisted by an
ardent one-armed revolutionary called Michael Davitt, who
had been imprisoned for his Fenian activities but was released
from penal servitude in England in 1877. He came back to Ireland at a critical time, just when the comparative prosperity of
Irish agriculture which had followed the Famine was about to
be dealt a severe blow by a sudden drop in world food prices.
All the old animosities of tenant against landlord flared up
again, as the small farmers found themselves unable to meet
the rent; and Michael Davitt was quick to exploit them. In
1879 he founded the Irish National Land League. At a League
Convention in August of that year, Davitt made it quite clear
that his aim was land nationalisation:

'The land of Ireland belongs to the people of Ireland, to
be held and cultivated for the sustenance of those whom
God declared to be inhabitants thereof. Land being created
to supply mankind with the necessities of existence, those
who cultivate it to that end have a higher claim to its absolute possession than those who make it an article of barter,

to be used or disposed of for profit or pleasure. The end for which the land of a country is created requires an equitable distribution of the same among the people who live upon the fruits of their labour in its cultivation.'

That there was a serious situation cannot be denied. There had been an economic crisis in the winter of 1878–9, with falling prices, crop failures and dreadful weather, which threatened the tenant farmers with the direst consequences—bankruptcy, eviction, starvation—that might echo the disaster of the Great Famine. Davitt, and later Parnell, used the Land League as a militant organisation, uniting all shades of nationalist opinion, to promote concerted agitation in defence of the threatened farmers.

The conventional picture of this time is of huge estates in Ireland predominantly owned by Protestant landlords, frequently absentee, who were living in idle luxury off the rents. They had the power to raise these rents or evict their tenants at will; the tenants had no rights at all. A tenant who improved his land would have the rent raised, because of the improvement, to a level he could not afford, and the landlord would install a new tenant who could. But this picture is one-sided; the rents, it seems, were never high enough to service the estates properly, according to modern historians, but it was a hugely emotional issue in Ireland at the time.

Parnell became president of the Land League, with Davitt as its organiser, and together they harnessed the ancient passions of the dispossessed Irish, the landless Irish, against the Establishment. Their aim was to reduce rents (by witholding them if necessary), to prevent evictions for non-payment, and ultimately to get the land back into native hands. And it was now that Parnell dreamed up a tactic that was to give the English language a new word. In 1880, a certain Captain Charles Boycott, of Lough Mask House, County Mayo, agent for Lord Erne, defied the Land League by refusing a tenant's request for a reduction of rent, intending to evict him for a more amenable tenant. Parnell had laid the ground for dealing with just such a situation in a significant speech in County Clare:

> 'Now what are you to do to a tenant who bids for a farm from which his neighbour has been evicted?' (*'Kill him! Shoot him!'*)
>
> 'Now I think I heard someone say "Shoot him"?' (*'Yes, that's right!'*)
>
> 'But I wish to point out to you a very much better way— a more Christian and charitable way, which will give the lost sinner an opportunity of repenting. When a man takes a farm from which another has been evicted, you must show him on the roadside when you meet him, you must show him in the fair and in the market-place, and even in the house of worship, by leaving him severely alone, by putting him into a moral Coventry, by isolating him from his kind as if he were a leper of old—you must show him your detestation of the crime he has committed, and you may depend upon it that there will be no man so full of avarice, so lost to shame, as to dare the public opinion of all right-thinking men and to transgress your unwritten code of laws.'

Thus was the 'boycott' born; and so severe was it that Captain Boycott and his family had to be rescued by troops, while volunteer Orange labourers from Ulster harvested his crops for him after his own workmen had all deserted.

The Boycott incident was only one of a series of combative confrontations in the so-called 'Land War' of 1879–82. It was a great mass movement of popular opinion, with demonstrations against evictions and a highly-organised relief agency to care for the families of those evicted or sent to prison.

The government, now headed once again by Gladstone, answered the Land League's challenge by passing a Coercion Bill, even though the Land League was itself technically a lawful organisation. And then in 1881, he pushed through a new Land Act, based on the principle of the 'three F's—Fixity of tenure, Fair rents, and Free sale'. New government tribunals, or land courts, were set up for fixing rents for a period of fifteen years. The old power of the landlord was forever taken away, and a system of dual ownership of the land came into being.

Even these measures were not enough for the Land League, which was demanding full peasant ownership of the land. The violence and outrages that broke out gave the government deep concern. Lord Cowper reported to the Cabinet:

'The state of the country is undoubtedly most serious. Nor do the number of outrages by any means represent the [gravity of the situation], and for this reason: that in many places . . . those who would profit [by outrages] are complete masters of the situation, and their temptation, therefore, is removed. Nobody dares to evict. Tenants of evicted farms, even those who have been in possession for more than a year, are daily giving them up. Eighty persons are under police protection. We cannot yet say for certain how far the autumn rents will be paid, but it appears already that in many places tenants have refused to pay more than Government valuation. Landlords will not agree to this, they will evict, and then a great increase of outrages may be expected. It will then be too late to give us extra powers. If they are to be conferred, the decision must be come to at once.'

Gladstone responded by arresting the League leaders, including Parnell; but this only served to increase the violence. John Bright, who was then a member of the government, admitted failure:

'The suspension of the Habeas Corpus Act had been successful in the case of the Fenians; we supposed it would be

Impression of a post-famine eviction scene.

The great emigration to America during and after the famine.
Waterloo Docks, Liverpool.

LAND LEAGUE CRUELTY.

Unionist propaganda poster denouncing the Land League
and its use of 'the Boycott'.

Unionist crowds at the Ulster Convention at Balmoral,
Belfast, in 1892

PARNELL—Well, Pat, near finished?
PAT—The grave is just ready, and there is the headstone. Have you decided whether
     you will insert the word Liberal or Conservative in that space yet, Sir.
PARNELL—No, Pat.   I think if I could manage to get the two words in it would be
     a good thing

Cartoon from *The Pilot*, 1885, demonstrating Charles Stewart Parnell's
power as leader of the Irish Party in the Westminster Parliament.

Gladstone introducing the first Home Rule Bill in
the House of Commons, 1886

successful in the case of the Land League. That was the mistake. The League was a bigger organisation. It extended all over the country. The arrest of the leaders did not affect it: the local branches were too well organised. For every man who was arrested there was another ready to take his place. Our information was wrong. The conspiracy was more widespread and more deeply rooted than we were led to suppose. It was not a case for the suspension of the Habeas Corpus Act.

'I admit the policy was a failure, or, at least, not as successful as we anticipated it would be. But under the circumstances, in face of the representations of the Irish Government, it was impossible to avoid trying it. Remember, too, that if we had not passed a Coercion Act we could not have got a good Land Bill through. That was a consideration which weighed much with me, and I think with all of us.'

Six months after Parnell was imprisoned, he was released, the campaign of coercion was called off, and Gladstone and even the Conservatives introduced further Acts of Parliament that would, over the years, abolish the old landlordism and turn Ireland into a land of peasant proprietors. It was a turning point, although not all historians think the results were good, in the long term. It left Irish agriculture imprisoned in a peasant ownership that was profoundly conservative and badly under-capitalised. It stultified any possible progress. It was above all a victory for nationalist sentiment, but was it perhaps a pyrrhic victory? In the last few years, radical young historians have been questioning the validity of the sentiment. The hated landlords, they now assert, were just as much the victims of an agricultural system that had always been bedevilled by the politics of the past. The old attitudes are being re-examined, to such an extent that one young scholar engaged in an analysis of landlordism in a southern county recently wrote a paper with the provocative title of *Predatory Peasants and Downtrodden Landlords!* Changed days indeed!

The First Home Rule Bill

Whether or not an economic historian with the benefit of hindsight might deplore the fact, the fight for land reform had been won and Parnell was in the ascendant. He now turned his attention to the other major political theme in Ireland—Home Rule. The General Election of 1885 produced a Liberal majority in the House of Commons, with Gladstone back in power and Parnell at the head of a substantial number of Irish Home Rulers. And in 1886, Gladstone, true to his long-held convictions about 'justice for Ireland', produced a Home Rule for Ireland Bill:

> 'Mr Speaker: Something must be done, something is imperatively demanded from us, to restore to Ireland the first conditions of civil life—the liberty of every individual, and the confidence of the people in the law.
>
> 'The mainspring of law in England is felt by the people to be English; the mainspring of law in Scotland is felt by the people to be Scotch: but the mainspring of law in Ireland is not felt by the people to be Irish . . .
>
> 'The strong instincts of the Irish people require, not only that laws should be good, but that they should proceed from a congenial and native source, and besides being good laws, they should be their own laws.
>
> 'We seek the settlement of that question in the establishment of a Parliament sitting in Dublin, for the conduct of Irish, as distinct from Imperial, affairs. That is my postulate, from which I set out . . .
>
> 'The essential conditions of any plan are, that the unity of the Empire must not be placed in jeopardy, and next that there should be reasonable safeguards for the Protestant minority, especially in the Province of Ulster.

'But, Sir, I cannot allow it to be said, that a Protestant
minority in Ulster, or elsewhere, is to rule the question at
large for Ireland, when five-sixths of its chosen representatives are of one mind in this matter . . .

'We stand face to face with Irish nationality. Englishmen
are eminently English; Scotchmen are profoundly Scotch;
but the Irishman is still more profoundly Irish. Is this an
evil, in itself? Sir, I hold that it is not.

'I say boldly that if this measure pass under happy circumstances, I hope the day may come when Ireland will
have reason to look on this Act as for practical purposes her
own Magna Carta.

'I ask that we should practise what we have often
preached. I ask that we should learn to rely less upon
merely written stipulations, and more upon those better
stipulations which are written on the heart and mind of
man.'

The Conservatives opposed the Bill tooth and nail, chiefly
on the grounds that there were no safeguards in it for Protestant interests in Ulster. But it was his own party that let Gladstone down; some of the Liberals were ultimately more
concerned about the effect it would have on the Empire.
Joseph Chamberlain led the opposition to the Bill from the
radical left wing of the Liberal Party:

'This new programme of Mr Parnell's involves a greater
extension than anything we have hitherto known or understood by Home Rule; the powers he claims for his support in
Parliament are altogether beyond anything which exists in
the case of the State Legislatures of the American Union,
which has hitherto been the type and model of Irish de-
mands, and if this claim were conceded we might as well for
ever abandon all hope of maintaining a united kingdom.
We should establish within thirty miles of our shores a new
foreign country animated from the outset with unfriendly

intentions towards ourselves. Such a policy as that, I firmly believe, would be disastrous and ruinous to Ireland herself. It would be dangerous to the security of this country, and under these circumstances I hold that we are bound to take every step in our power to avert so great a calamity.'

In the Commons, Gladstone fought hard to save his Home Rule Bill:

'Ireland stands at your bar expectant, hopeful, almost suppliant. Her words are the words of truth and soberness. She asks a blessed oblivion of the past, and in that oblivion our interest is deeper than ever hers. My Right Hon. friend the Member for East Edinburgh (Mr Goschen) asks us to-night to abide by the traditions of which we are the heirs. What traditions? By the Irish traditions? Go into the length and breadth of the world, ransack the literature of all countries, find, if you can, a single voice, a single book . . . in which the conduct of England towards Ireland is anywhere treated except with profound and bitter condemnation. Are these the traditions by which we are exhorted to stand? No; they are a sad exception to the glory of our country. They are a broad and black blot upon the pages of its history; and what we want to do is stand by the traditions of which we are the heirs in all matters except our relations with Ireland . . .'

Eventually, however, the Bill was defeated by thirty votes in the Commons and Gladstone lost office. He remained totally committed to the idea of Home Rule for Ireland, and so did Parnell. There seemed every reason to suppose that a resolute re-introduction of the Bill, as Gladstone planned on his return to office, would succeed next time. Ireland seemed poised on the brink of a solution to one of her most intractable problems—and the ensuing course of Irish history would surely have been very different.

But then, with success almost within their grasp, came

tragedy—tragedy for Parnell, at any rate. In November, 1890, a former member of Parnell's Irish Home Rule party, Captain William Henry O'Shea, named Parnell as co-respondent in a divorce suit against his wife. Parnell made no attempt to defend the suit. And suddenly, the ground of his pre-eminence began to crumble beneath his feet.

The Fall of Parnell

The fall of Parnell has become as much a part of Irish mythology as the fall of Icarus, whose arrogance tempted him to fly too close to the sun. W. B. Yeats, as much as anyone, was responsible for the creation of the myth, with his memorable couplet:

> 'The Bishops and the Party
> That tragic story made.'

Yeats saw Parnell as the romantic hero, the strong man standing alone being pulled down by a howling mob led by bishops and priests: a savage punishment for having dared to be the Protestant leader of what many Irishmen wanted to be an exclusively Catholic nationalism. But this was a purely literary invention, as remote from reality as the folk ballads about the past. Parnell had no one to blame but himself; and in point of fact the last people who turned on him were the prelates of the Catholic Church. The course of events is perfectly clear for those who choose to follow it.

Despite the clear evidence of Parnell's adultery, his party was at first solidly behind him, and issued several public statements in the days immediately following the divorce court verdict. One came in a telegram from a group of Irish MPs on a visit to America:

> 'We stand firmly by the leadership of the man who has brought the Irish people through unparalleled difficulties

and dangers, from servitude and despair to the very threshold of emancipation, with a genius, courage, and success
unequalled in our history. We do so, not only on the ground
of gratitude for those imperishable services in the past, but
in the profound conviction that Parnell's statesmanship
and matchless qualities as a leader are essential to the safety
of our cause.'

The Catholic hierarchy meanwhile maintained a strict
silence on the issue. It was Gladstone himself, as leader of the
English Liberals, who played the decisive part. In England,
Nonconformists had reacted most violently to the news of
Parnell's adultery. The Nonconformists had been the very
people who had been most ardent in support of Gladstone's
impeccably *moral* stand on the natural justice of Ireland's case
for Home Rule. Gladstone now feared that the Liberal Party
could not survive without their votes. And so, on the day
before the Irish Parliamentary Party met in the House of
Commons to re-elect Parnell as their leader, Gladstone delivered an ultimatum for Parnell in a letter to the Liberal
Chief Whip, Mr Morley:

'. . . While clinging to the hope of communication from
Mr Parnell to whomsoever addressed, I thought it necessary, viewing the arrangements for the commencement of
the session tomorrow, to acquaint Mr McCarthy with the
conclusion at which, after using all the means of observation and reflection in my power, I had myself arrived. It
was that, notwithstanding the splendid services rendered by
Mr Parnell to his country, his continuance at the present
moment in the leadership would be productive of consequences disastrous in the highest degree to the cause of Ireland.

'I think I may be warranted in asking you so far to
expand the conclusion I have given above as to add that the
continuance I speak of would not only place many hearty
and effective friends of the Irish cause in a position of great

embarrassment, but would render my retention of the leadership of the Liberal Party, based as it has been mainly upon the presentation of the Irish cause, almost a nullity.'

But this ultimatum did not reach the Irish Party members until after their meeting, when Parnell had been confirmed as leader, and so Gladstone promptly published his letter. Gladstone felt he had no choice, politically, and Parnell's Irish Party now felt they had no choice, either. They realised that Gladstone was their only chance of achieving Home Rule, and they opted for that instead of for loyalty to a discredited leader. It was only then that the Catholic bishops spoke on the moral issue; by then they, too, had no choice. For a year, Parnell fought desperately to regain his leadership. Many in his party still supported him, despite any moral indignation they might feel over the divorce and Parnell's subsequent marriage to Katherine O'Shea; they resented the fact that an English politician had interfered with an internal Irish question. But Parnell was now too discredited, and in October 1891 he died. It was a sad and sorry end to a great political career.

To all intents and purposes, it was the end of the Home Rule hopes for Ireland, even though the indomitable Gladstone produced a second Home Rule Bill in 1893; this one passed the Commons, but was overwhelmingly crushed by the House of Lords.

It was on that occasion that the voice of the Orangemen of Ulster was clearly heard, implacably opposed to any form of Home Rule, in the resolutions passed at an Orange demonstration on 12 July 1893:

'Resolution 1. We the Orangemen of the Loyal Orange District of Fivemiletown in the Co. of Tyrone assembled to celebrate the 203 anniversary of the memorable Victory gained at the Boyne by King William the Third of glorious memory hereby declare our steadfast adherence to the principles of civil and religious liberty thereby established in these realms, and our first determination to lay down our lives in their defence rather than allow them to be wrested from us.

'Resolution 2. In common with our loyalist fellow subjects in England and Scotland as well as in Ireland we deprecate the insidious and profligate and unpatriotic attempt now being made by a self seeking and reckless old politician abetted by a motley and heterogeneous rabble of professional agitators to smuggle through the House of Commons, with[out] the necessary full debate of its provisions a measure calculated to uproot the Constitution under which we live and to imperil our lives, our liberties and our worldly substance.

'Resolution 3. Lastly we would record our undying allegiance to the Gracious Monarch who has so long and so wisely wielded the sceptre over the Mighty Empire of which Ireland forms an integral part, our ardent attachment to the Constitution of the United Kingdom, and our fixed resolve never to submit to laws enacted by an Irish Parliament of which the members would be the nominees and puppets of the Roman Priesthood.'

In less than a century, the wheel had turned full circle. The Ulster Protestants who had so vigorously opposed the Act of Union in 1800 were now full-blooded Unionists. The Catholic masses who had supported the Act of Union with its implicit promise of complete Emancipation were now against it. And although the Home Rule issue would now lie dormant for a time, nationalism would burst into strident and ultimately bloody life again after the turn of the century, culminating in the trauma of the Easter Rising of 1916.

PART IV

A House Divided:
1891-1921

The more I enquired about attitudes to Irish history, and the
closer we got to modern times, the more I realised how hard it
is to be dispassionate about it. Objectivity, in Ireland, takes
long centuries to mature. No doubt the Irish now take a
reasonably detached view about the first Stone Age settlers
who came to Ireland around 7000 BC. Most have probably
come to terms with the iron-armed Celts from Central Europe
who moved in before the start of the Christian era, and set Ireland on a course of Celtic Christianity whose monks were
born adventurers and whose saints were all heroic. Even the
Vikings, my ancestors, who pulled Ireland somewhat roughly
into the mainstream of European action, are now thought of
as being almost respectable. That has taken a thousand years.
Maybe it will be another thousand years before the next wave
of incomers, the Anglo-Normans, will be found acceptable.

So how long will it take before we can put into proper per-
spective the period we will be covering in this fourth and final
section—the thirty years between the death of Charles
Stewart Parnell in 1891 and the Partition of Ireland in 1921?
1921 was the great watershed in modern Irish history, the key
event that set the present bounds of Ireland's political geo-
graphy. But it did much more than create a future; it also
created a past, by validating an exclusive view of history in
terms of 1921. It legitimised retrospectively the use of violence
by celebrating it as the only successful factor in the ultimate
victory; and thereby it touched a deeply responsive chord in a

people who have been described as more ready than most to indulge in violence for political ends.

I realise that I am treading dangerous ground now. Every country, every nation, every tribe has its own mythology which passes for history. Pride requires us all to transform our failures into triumphs. Any attempt to demythologise our historical ideology breeds irritation, if not downright resentment: try telling a British pub audience that Britain did not win the last war, it was America and Russia who won it for them! But what do you put in the place of historical mythology? The Republic of Ireland must be one of the few nations in the modern world where a distinguished politician like Dr Conor Cruise O'Brien can lose his seat in Parliament not, according to some, because of his political policies, but because he dared to try to popularise a revisionist version of history. In Ireland, even a Historiographical Revolution can have its victims.

The Gaelic Athletic Association and the Gaelic League

The highlights of the period we are covering in this final section are luridly illuminated: the revolt of the Unionists in Ulster that almost became open rebellion; the abortive Easter Rising in 1916 that led to the Sinn Féin victory at the polls in 1918; and the celebrated 'Troubles' that led to the Partition of Ireland. These are the familiar, perhaps too familiar, peaks that command the attention of patriot and historian alike. But they did not just happen as isolated bursts of frenetic activity. In all history, there is always a long, slow-burning fuse that can be traced as it leads towards an explosion.

In Ireland, during the twenty years from Parnell's death in 1891 to, say, 1911, I think we can detect two such fuses; or at any rate two strands, which can be characterised as the parliamentary strand and the revolutionary strand. The difference is clearly reflected in two seemingly innocuous organisations which flourished in Ireland in the years after Parnell's death. One was physical, the other was cultural; both were intensely and self-consciously nationalistic; and both represented a deliberate Celtic challenge to Anglo-Saxon ascendancy: the Gaelic Athletic Association and the Gaelic League.

The Gaelic Athletic Association was founded in 1884 by a sporting enthusiast called Michael Cusack, a large and formidable character who was immortalised as 'the Citizen' in James Joyce's *Ulysses*. It quickly became a mass movement, a patriotic assertion of national identity, by reviving traditional Irish sports like hurling and Gaelic football. It was essentially Catholic in its membership. The first patron of the Association, Archbishop Croke, expressed its aims unequivocally:

'One of the most painful and at the same time, one of the most frequently recurring reflections that, as an Irishman, I am compelled to make is that we are daily importing from England her fashions, her accents, her vicious literature, her music, her dances, and her manifold mannerisms, her games also and her pastimes, to the utter discredit of our own great national sports.

'Indeed, if we continue travelling for the next score years in the same direction that we have been going in for some time past, condemning the sports that were practised by our forefathers, effacing our national features as though we were ashamed of them, and putting on, with England's stuffs and broadcloths her masher habits, and such other effeminate follies as she may recommend, we had better at once, and publicly, abjure our nationality.'

The Gaelic Athletic Association was avowedly non-political in intention. But at least four of the original seven men who founded it were Fenians, and its uncompromising hostility to all foreign sports—the games of the Protestant incomers, in effect—made it overwhelmingly Catholic. It became a sort of badge of nationalist virility, and would hold mass parades whose participants carried hurleys, like weapons. It was viewed with considerable suspicion by the Royal Irish Constabulary, who saw it as a secret recruiting-ground for young revolutionaries.

The Gaelic League was also avowedly non-political, and for a long time succeeded in remaining so. But it was also effectively non-sectarian, and attracted Catholics and Protestants alike. What united them was a passionate concern for nationhood as expressed through the Gaelic language, a feeling that the loss of the ancient Irish language amounted to a loss of Irish identity. Its founding father was a language scholar called Douglas Hyde, the son of a Protestant Church of Ireland rector in County Roscommon. Because of illness in youth he missed the normal Protestant schooling, and was exposed instead to the influence of the local peasant children, from whom he discovered for himself the Irish vernacular. He had no overt political leanings, although he was later to become the first President of Eire in 1938; his interest in Irish culture was essentially romantic, an attempt to rediscover a cultural heritage before it was lost for ever, because the number of native speakers of Irish had been dwindling sharply throughout the century. Hyde's credo was expressed in a lecture entitled *The Necessity for de-Anglicising Ireland*:

'I should like to call attention to the illogical position of men who drop their own language to speak English, of men who translate their euphonious Irish names into English monosyllables, of men who read English books and know nothing about Gaelic literature, nevertheless protesting as a matter of sentiment that they hate the country which at every hand's turn they rush to imitate.'

Although Douglas Hyde wanted the movement to remain non-political, it could not stay impervious to the political climate of Ireland in the early years of the twentieth century. Gradually, the ultra-separatists began to take over the Gaelic League. In 1915, at a convention held in Dundalk, a resolution was adopted inserting in the stated aims of the League a clause that the League was working for a free Ireland. Dr Hyde, the League's President, resigned the following day, abandoning to the political extremists the movement he had founded:

'My ambition had always been to use the language as a neutral field upon which all Irishmen might meet . . . I was fighting English influence in a really effectual way . . . We were doing the only business that really counted, we were keeping Ireland Irish, and that in a way that the Government and the Unionists, though they hated it, were powerless to oppose. So long as we remained non-political there was no end to what we could do.'

What the League did achieve, in fact, was very considerable. At every level it propagated national self-reliance and self-respect. It fostered native industries, it introduced Gaelic into every branch of education, it turned St Patrick's Day into a national holiday. At its peak it had more than six hundred branches throughout Ireland, sold more than a quarter of a million publications a year, and employed a score of people full-time. It was much the most effective and well-organised national pressure group in Ireland around the turn of the century.

Perhaps this was because political activity in Ireland, after the death of Parnell and the demise of hopes for the early achievement of Home Rule, was in the doldrums. The forces which Parnell had unified into a national movement splintered into bickering groups after his fall. Perhaps the Gaelic League offered to many people a valid alternative to politics, in line with the new-look nationalisms that were evident everywhere in Europe, from Scandinavia to Hungary and Greece—movements that all sought to assert separate national and ethnic identities.

The Gaelic movement influenced a great literary revival in Ireland led by W. B. Yeats, 'A. E.', J. M. Synge and others. This reached a far wider audience—indeed, an international audience—because it was in English; and because so many of them were intensely politically minded, it gave an intellectual and literary cachet to the cause of Irish nationalism. It drew its inspiration from the romantic legends of ancient Ireland, tales of larger-than-life heroes like Cuchulainn, who were believed to have served their mistress Ireland with chivalrous self-sacrifice.

Sinn Féin and the Orange Order

At the formal political level, the Irish Party in the House of Commons, which represented the ideal of Home Rule through parliamentary activity, was beginning to bandage the wounds of the internal divisions that had torn it apart after the fall of Parnell. It entered the twentieth century unified and reinvigorated under the leadership of one of the most impressive of Parnell's followers, John Redmond, himself a highly skilled and effective parliamentarian. His opposition to the Act of Union of a century earlier was uncompromising:

> 'The Act of Union has no binding moral or legal force. We regard it as our fathers regarded it before us, as a great criminal act of usurpation carried by violence and fraud, and we say that no lapse of time and no mitigation of its details can ever make it binding upon our honour or our conscience.'

But the Home Rule revival did not satisfy everyone. Although the IRB, the old Irish Republican Brotherhood, was to all intents and purposes dormant, there were still plenty of activists in the wings longing for complete separation from England by any means. These revolutionary elements found their natural leader in a brilliant young journalist called Arthur Griffith, who edited a new weekly paper called *United Irishman* from its foundation in 1899. Griffith advocated not armed insurrection (which most people realised would be futile at that time) but an advanced form of Parnell's obstructionism—a general boycott, in effect, on all forms of parliamentarianism:

> 'We call upon our countrymen to withdraw all assistance from the promoters of a useless, degrading and demoralising policy; and, refusing to attend the British Parliament or to recognise its right to legislate for Ireland, to remain at home to help in promoting Ireland's interests and to aid in guarding its national rights.'

Under Griffith's guidance, the various small activist groups came together in 1908 to form a new political organisation called Sinn Féin. The words Sinn Féin mean 'We Ourselves'; its purpose was stated unequivocally in its constitution: 'The object of Sinn Féin is to re-establish the Independence of Ireland.' The boycott was to be a positive one: Irish Members of Parliament should set up an assembly in Dublin, there should be an independent Irish civil service, a separate merchant navy, a separate system of law courts, and so on.

It was not full-blooded republicanism yet, although that was what it would eventually lead to, and the name Sinn Féin would become ominously familiar in Britain in the years to come. But for the time being the political initiative was still with the parliamentary Home Rulers—especially when the General Election of 1910 made the Liberal government at Westminster dependent on the support of the Irish Party MPs. The achievement of Home Rule now seemed, at long last, merely a formality, a matter only of time.

In the north, the prospect of Home Rule had always filled the Ulster Unionists and their MPs with dismay, even horror. The Irish Unionist movement was as powerfully motivated, in its way, as the nationalist Home Rule movement in the south. It was supported almost exclusively by Irish Protestants of Anglo-Irish or Scottish-Irish descent, who comprised roughly twenty-five per cent of the population of the whole of Ireland. They opposed Home Rule because they wanted to continue the dominance in public life they had enjoyed for centuries; under a predominantly Catholic Home Rule parliament in Dublin they feared not only social and economic disaster, but also a threat to their own civil and religious liberties. Their basic argument, in a statement to Gladstone by the earliest Unionist organisation, the Irish Loyal and Patriotic Union, in 1886, had been that the Union had brought immense benefits to Ireland:

'We but repeat, what is well known to every one who has bestowed attention on the subject, that, in every detail which goes to make up the sum of civilised life, the Irish people are at this moment very far in advance of the condition of their ancestors at the time of the Union. They are better housed, better clad, better fed; they receive better prices for the produce of their farms, and higher wages for their labour; they have greater liberty and better protection in health, abundant provision for sickness, and facilities for the education and advancement in life of their children, such as were undreamt of eighty years ago. No measure has been passed, since the Union, for the benefit of the English or the Scotch people, in which they have not shared; and many Acts have been passed specially for their benefit which have not been extended to Scotland or England. These are facts which cannot be controverted, and which no one, except hireling agitators, would attempt to deny or distort.'

Gladstone and his Liberals had been the Unionists' bogeymen. Ulster had been profoundly suspicious of the Liberal Party ever since the days of his Home Rule Bills in 1886 and 1893. The Unionists had powerful allies in the British Conservative Party, which had declared itself totally opposed to Home Rule and even took the name of Unionist itself, but the prospect of another Liberal government was always viewed as a threat.

——— Boundary of the present division of
the 'six counties of Ulster'

In the aftermath of the 1886 Home Rule Bill, Lord Randolph Churchill had come to Belfast to pledge total Conservative support to the Ulster Protestants; and during that visit he had given the Unionists a slogan which became the war cry of a suddenly revitalised Orange Order: 'Ulster will fight; Ulster will be right!'

Lord Randolph Churchill had let drop the remark that 'The Orange card is the card to play,' and the Orange Order was not slow to fill the role thus offered to it. It had never been much of a force since its foundation in 1795, but in the 1880s it suddenly became respectable, a rallying point for all classes; and now, too, the threat of physical violence was no longer confined to the revolutionaries of the south. There had been riots in the streets of Belfast in 1886 as Protestant and

Catholic workmen clashed. And when Gladstone's second Home Rule Bill was in preparation in 1892, the Orange card was played again in a huge Ulster Convention League demonstration in Belfast at which 12,000 delegates carried an ominous resolution:

'We solemnly resolve and declare that we express the devoted loyalty of Ulster Unionists to the crown and constitution of the United Kingdom; that we avow our fixed resolve to retain unchanged our present position as an integral part of the United Kingdom; that we declare to the people of Great Britain our conviction that the attempt to set up such an all-Irish Parliament will result in disorder, violence and bloodshed.'

The threat to Unionism had been averted when the House of Lords threw out the second Home Rule Bill in 1893. But the Unionists knew it would only be a temporary reprieve, and set about trying to impress their case on public opinion on the mainland. The Liberals came back to office in 1906 with a landslide victory; and for the next General Election, in 1910, the Irish Unionist Alliance published a *Manifesto to the electors of Great Britain* which summarised their standpoint clearly:

'One million five hundred thousand of your fellow subjects in Ireland, that is to say, about one-third of the whole population of the country, call for your help at the polls. They are loyally devoted to the Legislative Union between Great Britain and Ireland under which they have been born and lived. They include, beside many thousands of scattered Royalists in the West and South of Ireland, the overwhelming majority of the most progressive and prosperous parts of Ulster, including the great city of Belfast. They comprise Episcopalians, Presbyterians, Methodists, and other religious persuasions including a minority of loyal Roman Catholics. Be assured that they know from

experience the danger under Home Rule of religious, social
and political tyranny from the men who have been the enemies of Great Britain. We are convinced that the injury
caused by Home Rule to the great industries of the North
and other parts of Ireland would send thousands of workmen to your shores competing with you for employment
and adding to the existing mass of unemployed . . . We are
certain that a country within a few miles of you governed
by those who have shown their hostility to Great Britain
may constitute, especially at the present time, a standing
menace to you from a naval and military point of view . . .'

In that 1910 election, the Liberals lost their overall
majority, and had to rely on the support of the Irish Parliamentary Party at Westminster. When the House of Lords
threw out the Liberal Finance Bill before the election—in effect, the Budget—the Liberals after re-election pushed
through a measure to curb the Lords; henceforth the Lords
would only be able to delay a Bill, not reject it. The way was
now open for another Home Rule Bill which would command
a majority in the House of Commons without the fail-safe of
the Lords—and Ulster braced itself for the struggle.

The Third Home Rule Bill, 1912–14

As so often happens in history, the moment and the mood produced the man. In 1910 the Irish Unionist Party had chosen a
new leader. His name was Edward Carson, a Dublin-born
barrister of compelling presence and ruthless ability, as Oscar
Wilde had learned to his cost during his celebrated cross-
examination in court. Carson was Unionist MP for Dublin
University, a tall, forbidding, saturnine figure, who wanted to
preserve the Union, and it was largely due to his aggressive,
well-organised opposition to Home Rule that Ulster was
'saved' for Unionism in the fateful years of 1912 to 1914.

Carson went on the offensive right away. In 1911, when the Parliament Act curbing the House of Lords was passed, he held a mass meeting in Belfast at which he laid down the implacable line that was to be followed:

> 'We must be prepared, in the event of a Home Rule Bill passing, with such measures as will carry on for ourselves the government of those districts of which we have control. We must be prepared . . . the morning Home Rule passes, ourselves to become responsible for the government of the Protestant province of Ulster.'

The political emphasis on 'Protestant' was very deliberate. Modern historians now see the first decade of the twentieth century as a period when southern Ireland came more and more under the influence, even control, of the Catholic hierarchy. Severe, even punitive restrictions were being imposed on Catholics throughout Ireland, over mixed marriages, for instance. The power of the Catholic Church was growing ominously, and Protestants in the north were alarmed that *Home* Rule would in effect mean *Rome* Rule. In the event, after the South became independent in 1921, its first Constitution showed that these fears had not been completely groundless. It helps to explain the ferocity with which the Protestants were prepared to defend themselves against a Catholic Ascendancy which might succeed the Protestant Ascendancy they themselves had once enjoyed.

When the Home Rule Bill was about to be introduced, in April 1912, the new leader of the Conservative Opposition, Andrew Bonar Law, came to Belfast. He was of Ulster stock himself, and he rallied the 100,000 Ulstermen at his mass meeting by appealing to their historical consciousness, recalling the siege of Londonderry in 1689 when the Protestants held out against King James II:

> 'Once again you hold the pass for the Empire. You are a besieged city, and you have closed the gates. Does not the

picture of the past, the glorious past with which you are so familiar, rise again before your eyes? The Government by their Parliament Act have erected a boom against you, a boom to cut you off from the help of the British people. You will burst that boom.'

The actual Home Rule Bill, when it was unveiled two days later by the Liberal Prime Minister, Herbert Asquith, in the House of Commons, seemed rather a mild document compared with the belligerent rodomontade that had been prepared for it. The Irish Parliament would only have limited internal jurisdiction; Westminster would control policy on defence, peace or war, relations with the crown, even the police, and it would retain effective control of the revenue. But Carson knew it was only the thin edge of the wedge, and the Unionist Anti-Home Rule campaign was stepped up. On 28 September 1912 Carson led a huge concourse of defiant Ulstermen in signing a Solemn League and Covenant. There were 218,000 signatories—and some even signed in their own blood:

'Being convinced in our consciences that Home Rule would be disastrous to the material well-being of Ulster as well as of the whole of Ireland, subversive of our civil and religious freedom, destructive of our citizenship and perilous to the unity of the Empire, we, whose names are underwritten, men of Ulster, loyal subjects of His Gracious Majesty, King George V, humbly relying on the God whom our fathers in days of stress and trial confidently trusted, do hereby pledge ourselves in solemn Covenant throughout this our time of threatened calamity to stand by one another in defending for ourselves and our children our cherished position of equal citizenship in the United Kingdom and in using all means which may be found necessary to defeat the present conspiracy to set up a Home Rule Parliament in Ireland. And in the event of such a Parliament being forced upon us we further solemnly and mutually pledge ourselves to refuse to recognise its authority. In sure confidence that God will defend the right we hereto subscribe our names.'

On the quayside at Belfast, as he was setting off for London after the signing of the Solemn League and Covenant, Edward Carson spoke to his massed supporters:

'Today we have put our enemies into such a difficulty that they are thinking, "What on earth are we going to do?" Well, I can tell you one thing they had better *not* do, and that is to interfere with Belfast! We are quite satisfied to remain as we are under a United Parliament. But we will never have Home Rule; and I do not envy any number of Governments which try to come here and force it down our throats!'

This was no idle threat. The Ulstermen were already practising drill in military style. Early in 1913, the Ulster Unionist Council formed an organised Ulster Volunteer Force of 100,000 men. A few years later, Lord Dunleath of County Down wrote a memorandum to Carson recalling the way in which the UVF had been formed:

'We felt that it was the plain duty of those of us who were possessed of influence to take some step, which would convince the Government of the reality of our determination to resist this policy by every means in our power, and at the same time to attract to Ulster the attention of the masses in England and Scotland. We commenced by drilling our Orangemen and our Unionist Clubs, wherever drill instructors could be obtained, and suitable halls and lodges were available. Later on we amalgamated these forces, organised them into Companies and Battalions, appointed officers and section leaders, and gradually equipped and trained them into a very fairly efficient force of volunteer infantry. Finally we succeeded in providing them with a good supply of arms and ammunition.

'We can certainly claim that we have succeeded in turning the attention of Englishmen and Scotchmen towards Ulster and its inhabitants; we can also claim that the existence of this large armed force of Volunteers has materially assisted our political leaders, and that it will continue to assist them in the future.'

Not to be outdone, the nationalists in the south founded the Irish Volunteers, and at Westminster the parliamentary battle over the Home Rule Bill raged unabated. All attempts to reach a compromise between north and south failed, and eventually Asquith, the Liberal leader, came to fear that Carson would declare a UDI with a provisional government in Belfast. So acute was the crisis that Asquith even contemplated ordering the British troops stationed at the Curragh near Dublin to move into the north. It would have been a step of the utmost gravity. Disturbed at the prospect of being ordered to 'coerce' Ulster and take arms against the Ulster Volunteers, fifty-eight British officers at the Curragh proffered their resignations. It was not quite a mutiny; but it showed Asquith that he could not rely on the loyalty of the Army to quell Ulster and he drew back from the brink.

The following month, in April 1914, as if to underline the government's helplessness, a Unionist agent landed at Larne a shipment of 35,000 rifles and five million rounds of ammunition which had been purchased in Germany. The Irish Volunteers retaliated with some gun-running of their own, which they carried out in broad daylight, at Howth on the north side of Dublin Bay.

It seemed now that the twin slow-burning fuses were hastening along the last few inches before the powder-keg went up. The Home Rule Bill had been duly passed and placed on the Statute Book. A conference between the two sides at Buckingham Palace late in July ended in deadlock. Ireland was now divided into two heavily armed camps. John Redmond, the Irish Parliamentary Party leader, was rapidly

losing control of the Home Rule movement, and his Irish Volunteers were being infiltrated by revolutionaries. Civil war
seemed imminent. Then, on 4 August 1914, Britain and Germany went to war. In an agonisingly difficult decision, John
Redmond pledged Ireland's support for the war, as did
Edward Carson, and thousands of Irishmen from both north
and south enlisted with the British forces. The Home Rule Act
was shelved until such time as the war would be over, when
there would be special amending legislation for Ulster. For
Westminster, the Ulster crisis was over, or at least in abey-
ance; but in Ireland, nationalism was still very much a live
issue.

The Easter Rising

When the First World War began, there were three private
armies in the south of Ireland: the Irish Volunteers, nominally
controlled by John Redmond; the Citizen Army, led by the
Labour leader James Connolly, to defend the rights of the
workers; and the IRB, the secret Irish Republican Brotherhood, the extreme Fenian wing of the nationalists. It was
much the smallest of the groups, numbering only about two
thousand in 1914; but it was from the IRB, through a young
poet-schoolteacher called Patrick Pearse, that the spark
would come to ignite the celebrated Easter Rising of 1916.

Redmond's position as leader of the broad nationalist
movement had been severely affected by his decision to support Britain in the war. A nationalist jingle gained instant
popularity:

> Full steam ahead, John Redmond said
> that everything was well, chum;
> Home Rule will come when we are dead
> and buried out in Belgium.

Meanwhile, Arthur Griffith, the leader of the political Sinn

Féin party, pushed his stance on boycotting anything English
to its logical conclusion:

> 'Ireland is not at war with Germany. She has no quarrel
> with any continental power. England is at war with Ger-
> many, and Mr Redmond has offered England the services
> of the Volunteers to defend Ireland. What has Ireland to
> defend, and whom has she to defend it against?
>
> 'Our duty is in no doubt. We are Irish Nationalists, and
> the only duty we can have is to stand for Ireland's interests,
> irrespective of the interests of England, or Germany, or any
> other foreign country.'

The disenchantment with Redmond was echoed in a letter
written by a nationalist Ulsterwoman, Mabel McConnell, to
George Bernard Shaw in November 1914:

> 'Redmond is dead as a doornail in Ireland, I don't say
> this because he is a political opponent of the men I stand by;
> it is an absolute fact and any person familiar with Ireland at
> the moment, and honest, would tell you so; the country was
> more advanced nationally than he knew—than anyone
> knew—even the strongest separatist leaders—and he has
> sickened it. He still has a strong following, strong on paper
> and in sending paper resolutions to the Press, but the Irish
> volunteers are the only real force, Redmond's are dummies
> in almost every place and Redmond has now round him
> every corrupt force in Ireland, Hibernianism, the rottenest
> of the priests and gombeen men, the toadies and Shoneens,
> but every bit of brain and spirit is on the side of Ireland a
> Nation. We hear the same reports from every part where we
> have friends; the people are far sounder than anyone
> believed, not only have they scouted recruiting—as one old
> farmer here said to my husband the other day, he wouldn't
> send his dog to fight for England—but they have shrewdly
> sized up the Home Rule Bill and are quite unconcerned as
> to whether we ever get that impotent measure or not.'

George Bernard Shaw replied with characteristic insight and sagacity:

'Redmond may not be your ideal; but he is big enough to have done the right thing on this not very difficult occasion. In Ireland we have always suffered from a plague of clever fools always saying the wrong thing in the most skilful way. When you get a stupid man who says the right thing with rhetoric enough to make himself listened to, be thankful for him, and stand by him until you have somebody better to put in his place.'

To the men of the IRB, however, the arguments for or against John Redmond were irrelevant. They saw the outbreak of war as an opportunity and a challenge—a challenge to Fenian courage, and an opportunity to seize independence while England was embarrassed by foreign embroilments. Patrick Pearse expressed it very clearly:

'The European War has brought about a crisis which may contain, as yet hidden within it, the moment for which the generations have been waiting. It remains to be seen whether, if that moment reveals itself, we shall have the sight to see and the courage to do; or whether it shall be written of this generation, alone of all the generations of Ireland, that it had none among it who dared to make the ultimate sacrifice.'

Patrick Pearse himself had a mystical concept of nationalism, a highly-charged, romantic view of the exaltation of blood-sacrifice. At the annual commemoration of Theobald Wolfe Tone in 1913, he had yoked together politics and martyrdom in a soaring oration:

'To break the connection with England, the never-failing source of all our political evils, and to assert the independence of his country—those were his objects . . . Such is the high and sorrowful destiny of the heroes: to turn their

backs to the pleasant paths and their faces to the hard
paths, to blind their eyes to the fair things of life . . . and to
follow only the far, faint call that leads them into the battle
or to the harder death at the foot of a gibbet.'

It had the ring of Messianic prophecy; and Pearse became
obsessed with making the prophecy come true. In the very first
weeks of the war, the IRB resolved that a rising must take
place in Ireland sometime during the war, and a military
council was set up to plan it. Patrick Pearse was one of its
members, along with James Connolly; and it was Pearse, in
another funeral oration, who set the tone of the movement
with his apocalyptic view of nationalism:

'Life springs from death; and from the graves of patriot
men and women spring living nations. The Defenders of
this Realm have worked well in secret and in the open. They
think that they have pacified Ireland. They think that they
have purchased half of us and intimidated the other half.
They think that they have foreseen everything, think that
they have provided against everything; but the fools, the
fools, the fools!—they have left us our Fenian dead, and
while Ireland holds these graves, Ireland unfree shall never
be at peace.'

In his neurotic obsession with death and blood-sacrifice,
Pearse was very much a man of his time, a romantic like
Rupert Brooke and of that generation who went to war not to
kill the enemy but to die. To Pearse martyrdom was a sweet
and necessary thing to keep the fire of nationalism burning.
The passion of his oratory has haunted the Irish imagination
ever since; and it is this that has elevated him in folk-lore to
the position of chief saint of the events of 1916. Historians
now recognise, however, that he was the apostle of the Rising,
but not its organiser nor its leader.

It was in January 1916 that the Military Council of the
Irish Republican Brotherhood decided that the long-awaited

rising would take place that Easter. They would use James Connolly's small Citizen Army, and unbeknownst to the Chief of Staff of the Irish Volunteers, Eoin McNeill, they planned to exploit the Volunteers, too, who would be holding routine manoeuvres that Easter weekend. The plan was to supply the Volunteers with German arms that Sir Roger Casement was scheduled to bring from Germany that weekend, and thus draw them willy-nilly into the rising.

But everything that could go wrong did go wrong. On the Thursday before Easter, Eoin McNeill discovered the plot. He had consistently opposed any suggestion of a rebellion, and now, angered by this betrayal by his colleagues, he cancelled the planned manoeuvres. On Good Friday, however, he changed his mind, in view of the imminent arrival of the German arms. But the German arms never did arrive. The ship carrying them was intercepted by a British naval vessel and scuttled by its crew in Queenstown Harbour, taking the arms it carried down with it. Sir Roger Casement, trying to reach Ireland in time to warn the IRB leaders to call off the rising, was arrested as he came ashore from a German submarine and was subsequently executed for treason. So on Easter Sunday McNeill once again changed his orders: the manoeuvres would not take place after all. But the IRB conspirators refused to back down; they sent out the call to as many of their own men in the Citizen Army and the Volunteers as they could reach, and on Easter Monday, 24 April 1916, some 1,600 armed insurgents moved unopposed into several prominent buildings in the centre of Dublin.

Before the citizenry of Dublin, or the British Army for that matter, were properly aware of what was going on, Patrick Pearse was standing in front of the General Post Office building in O'Connell Street, reading aloud to a small group of puzzled bystanders the Proclamation of the Provisional Government of the Irish Republic:

'Irishmen and Irishwomen: In the name of God and of

132

the dead generations from which she receives her old tradition of nationhood, Ireland, through us, summons her children to her flag and strikes for her freedom.

'Having organised and trained her manhood through her secret revolutionary organisation, the Irish Republican Brotherhood, and through her open military organisations, the Irish Volunteers and the Irish Citizen Army, having patiently perfected her discipline, having resolutely waited for the right moment to reveal itself, she now seizes that moment, and supported by her exiled children in America and by gallant allies in Europe, but relying in the first on her own strength, she strikes in full confidence of victory.

'We declare the right of the people of Ireland to the ownership of Ireland, and to the unfettered control of Irish destinies, to be sovereign and indefeasible. The long usurpation of that right by a foreign people and government has not extinguished that right, nor can it ever be extinguished except by the destruction of the Irish people. In every generation the Irish people have asserted their right to national freedom and sovereignty: six times during the past three hundred years they have asserted it in arms. Standing on that fundamental right and again asserting it in arms in the face of the world, we hereby proclaim the Irish Republic as a Sovereign Independent State, and we pledge our lives and the lives of our comrades-in-arms to the cause of its freedom, of its welfare, and of its exaltation among the nations . . .

Signed on behalf of the Provisional Government,
Thomas J. Clarke

Sean Mac Diarmada	Thomas Mac Donagh
P. H. Pearse	Eamonn Ceannt
James Connolly	Joseph Plunkett'

The insurrection was doomed to failure from the start. The British government poured in troop reinforcements and systematically began to reduce the rebel positions. Although they were totally outnumbered and overwhelmed by the superior fire-power of the British troops, the insurgents held out fiercely. The normal life of Dublin was paralysed; 450 men, women and children were killed, over 2,600 wounded, while the Army lost 17 officers and 99 other ranks, with over 350 wounded. At last, five days after the start of the Rising, on Saturday, 29 April, the order was given to surrender:

> 'In order to prevent the further slaughter of Dublin citizens and in the hope of saving the lives of our followers now surrounded and hopelessly outnumbered . . . the Commandants of the various districts in the City and County will order their commands to lay down arms.'

Patrick Pearse had got the blood-sacrifice he wanted, in rich measure. But he and his colleagues had failed to stir the public to glorious revolution, as they had hoped; the public was merely angry at the insensate destruction and slaughter they had unleashed. The newspapers roundly condemned the Rising, and the crowds through which the ring-leaders were marched off to prison to await court martial were at times openly hostile. Public opinion in Britain, too, was predictably hostile, for the Rising was an open act of treachery in war time.

And yet, within a few days, Irish public opinion was swinging right around, the unpopular extremists had become popular heroes, and the Rising had become an inspiration for poets and patriots alike. It would wring from W. B. Yeats one of his most evocative and memorable lines:

> 'I write it out in a verse—
> MacDonagh and MacBride
> And Connolly and Pearse
> Now and in time to be,
> Wherever green is worn,
> Are changed, changed utterly:
> A terrible beauty is born.'

The immediate reason for this dramatic change was the court-martialling and subsequent execution of the ringleaders. No fewer than ninety prisoners were sentenced to death, although seventy-five of the sentences were commuted to penal servitude. Fifteen of the death sentences were, however, carried out, starting with Patrick Pearse, Tom Clarke and Thomas MacDonagh on Wednesday, May 3, four days after the surrender. Further executions were carried out on May 4, May 5, May 8, and May 12. Doubtless the military authorities had no option than the summary execution of men who had committed high treason; and public opinion in England would have stood for nothing less, at a time when British soldiers were being shot for desertion or for cowardice in the trenches.

But public opinion in Ireland reacted quite differently. As the secret courts martial and subsequent executions were announced in Dublin one after another, and rumours spread round the city like wildfire, Irish dislike of the Rising turned to shock and horror that, in the age-old phrase, Irish boys were being done to death at the hands of the British. The malefactors became martyrs—as Patrick Pearse had doubtless hoped.

Just how quickly the process happened is illustrated in a long letter from an unknown Dublin woman, written during and after the Rising, which prophesied with uncanny accuracy what would happen. She was against the Rising; but as the letter goes on, written in instalments day by day, the change of mood becomes strikingly apparent:

'Of course this is *not* Ireland's rebellion—only a Sinn Féin rising . . . How often have I laughed and quarrelled over the bare idea of an Irish Republic! It is so utterly un-Irish. Of course we want our own country free from foreign rule. But any one with sense must see that it must come by England's consent, not against England's will . . .

'The Sinn Féin leaders were such good men. They died

like saints. Oh! the pity of it! and Ireland wanted them so much! They were men of such beautiful character—such high literary power and attainments—mystics, who kept the light burning. What madness came over them! And they were so splendid for the language. They lived such pure lives—as the priests who shrived them before execution said "The clean pure lives—the absolute resignation—may they pray for us, not we for them." They have brought great and terrible trouble on us and Ireland—*but they meant to do the exact opposite.* They have crushed us under a weight of sorrow and shame—*but they meant the reverse.* What wild madness came over them!

'If you read, as I did, Pearse's letter written to his mother a few hours before he was shot—the beautiful courage—the utter resignation and the great love—and the heart break, for he knew what he had done to Ireland then! But he said, "I know and believe God will bring good out of all this to Ireland." But he also said, "Now they'll say hard things of us—they'll be angry—eventually they'll not." And we believe the first prophecy of the man who stood on the threshold of the next world—already we see it being fulfilled.

'But, as sure as God's sun rises in the East, if England doesn't get things right—if there's not immediately concili-ation, and love and mercy poured out on Ireland—all the Sinn Fein leaders will be canonised! For their own merits. You know how Ireland is always merciful to the dead.'

But there was not 'immediately conciliation'. And so the unlikely heroes of the Easter Rising joined the long litany of Irish warriors and martyrs and far-off battles long ago. The Rising had been transformed into an Ascension:

> Their dream had left me numb and cold,
> But yet my spirit rose in pride,
> Refashioning in burnished gold
> The images of those who died

Ulster Unionist propaganda postcard *c.* 1912 appealing to
British public opinion to maintain the Union.

The Ulster Volunteer Force in possession of Larne Harbour unloading arms
and ammunition bought from Germany in 1914 to defend Ulster against
Home Rule.

Patrick Henry Pearse by Sean O'Sullivan, RHA.

THE GRAPHIC

AN ILLUSTRATED WEEKLY NEWSPAPER

The entire contents of this paper, both Illustrations and Letterpress, are copyright.

No. 2413. Vol. XCIII.
Registered as a Newspaper.

SATURDAY, MAY 6, 1916

PRICE SIXPENCE
By Post, 7d.

The Battle of Dublin

SOLDIERS OPENING FIRE ON THE SINN FEINERS, WHO ARE SNIPING FROM HOUSES 200 YARDS AWAY

British soldiers in a Dublin street during the 1916 Easter uprising.

Sackville Street after being shelled by a British gun boat on the River Liffey during the 1916 Easter uprising.

Dáil Eireann 1919. Eamonn de Valera is in the centre of the front row.

Or were shut in the penal cell.
Here's to you, Pearse, your dream not mine,
But yet the thought for this you fell
Has turned life's waters into wine.

A. E.

Partition

The unexpected outcome of the Rising meant, in the first place, a total victory for the violent, Fenian tradition over the parliamentary, constitutional tradition in Irish politics led by John Redmond. There were other factors, too, such as the threat that Britain might enforce military conscription in Ireland to help the war effort, which drove countless young men to vote Sinn Fein at the polls. The mood in the south is vividly illustrated by a Unionist report on Sinn Féin activities in Cork in March 1917:

'The danger at present is this—the active Sinn Féiners are all young and intelligent men, generally teetotallers. Unlike the ordinary political fellows, they do not patronise public-houses and talk there over matters. They are silent and know how to keep their mouths closed, but they think and plot the more. Perhaps if they had a little latitude to let off steam at, say, a public meeting, it would act as a safety-valve. But the fact is they are—a great many of them—"brainy" in well-to-do positions; they speak little in public, and as in all secret political gatherings—suffering as they think under great wrongs—there is a danger of an outburst. Of course you know in Cork we always talk and do not act—that may be the case, but this silence on a matter which is deep in the hearts of thousands of young fellows in the city is to say the least very ugly and portends something more than usual happening unless they are pulled up in time.'

Just after the war ended, at the General Election of December 1918, Sinn Féin Republican candidates won a landslide victory over the Parliamentary Party, winning seventy-three seats against their six: in the north the Unionists won their usual block of twenty-six seats. Half of the victors were still in jail on various charges of subversion; but true to Sinn Féin's declared policy, the members refused to go to Westminster, and instead set up a National Assembly in Dublin—Dáil Eireann. The leader of Sinn Féin was now Eamonn de Valera, a commandant in the Easter Rising who had narrowly escaped the firing squad. De Valera had always been totally uncompromising in his demand for total independence:

'The only banner under which our freedom can be won at the present time is the Republican banner. It is as an Irish Republic that we have a chance of getting international recognition . . . Some might have faults to find with that and prefer other forms of government. But we are all united on this—that we want complete and absolute independence . . . This is the time to get freedom. Then we can settle by the most democratic means what particular form of government we may have. I only wish to say in reference to the last clause that there is no contemplation in it of having a monarchy in which the monarch would be of the House of Windsor.'

In January 1919 the Dáil met in Dublin; the Unionist MPs refused to attend, and the Sinn Féin members adopted a declaration of the Irish Republic in sympathy with that for which Pearse and his colleagues had died:

'The Irish people is by right a free people. And whereas English rule in this country is and always has been based upon force and fraud and maintained by military occupation against the declared will of the people; and whereas the Irish Republic was proclaimed in Dublin on Easter

Monday, 1916, by the Irish Republican Army acting on behalf of the Irish people; and whereas the Irish electorate has, in the General Election of December 1918 declared by an overwhelming majority its firm allegiance to the Irish Republic.

'Now therefore, we ratify the establishment of the Irish Republic and pledge ourselves and our people to make this declaration effective by every means at our command . . .

'In the name of the Irish people we humbly commit our destiny to Almighty God. We ask His divine blessing on this the last stage of the struggle which we have pledged ourselves to carry through to Freedom . . .'

Although Sinn Féin had hoped to achieve their ends by passive resistance, there was no holding the violent elements in the Volunteer force. The guerrillas concentrated their attacks on the Royal Irish Constabulary, with signal successes in the rural areas. The British government sent in reinforcements, the so-called Black and Tans—British mercenaries, in effect, some of them young veterans of the World War who had not settled to civilian life and now, as instant recruits for the Royal Irish Constabulary, tried to quell the Irish guerrillas by brutality and terror tactics. A British government spokesman issued an appropriately bland statement on the Black and Tans in 1920:

'They did not wait for the usual uniform, these Black and Tans who have joined the RIC. They came at once. They know what danger is. They have looked death in the eyes before and did not flinch. They will not flinch now. They will go on with the job—the job of making Ireland once again safe for the law-abiding, and an appropriate hell for those whose trade is agitation, and whose method is murder.'

The 'method' of the Black and Tans themselves could hardly be described as pacific, and there are countless folk memories of atrocities—on both sides. In March 1920 a jury in Cork found unanimously that the Lord Mayor had been deliberately murdered by the Black and Tans:

> 'We find that the late Alderman MacCurtain, Lord Mayor of Cork, died from shock and haemorrhage caused by bullet wounds, and that he was wilfully murdered under circumstances of the most callous brutality, and that the murder was organised and carried out by the Royal Irish Constabulary, officially directed by the British Government, and we return a verdict of wilful murder against David Lloyd George, Prime Minister of England; Lord French, Lord Lieutenant of Ireland; Ian MacPherson, late Chief Secretary of Ireland; Acting Inspector General Smith, of the Royal Irish Constabulary . . .'

The Irish Republican Army, the IRA, as the Irish Volunteers now called themselves, held their own, meeting violence with counter-violence; Sinn Féin tried to impose political control on the situation, but the gunmen said No; and so it goes on. Eventually, with both sides exhausted and sickened by the conflict, a truce was arranged in July 1921. 'The Troubles', as the war was euphemistically called, appeared to be over.

The ferocity of the Troubles had tended to divert attention from what was happening over Ulster. The guerrilla war in the south effectively prevented any political discussions about the Home Rule Act that had been shelved in 1914, so the Prime Minister, Lloyd George, decided on an imposed solution. Lloyd George clearly understood the deep-rooted fears of the Ulstermen about Home Rule:

> 'They are as alien in blood, in religious faith, in traditions, in outlook—as alien from the rest of Ireland in this respect as the inhabitants of Fife or Aberdeen . . . To place them under [Irish] national rule against their will would be as glaring an outrage on the principles of liberty and self-government as the denial of self-government would be for

the rest of Ireland.'

The Ulster Unionists had never wanted Partition, nor did they want a separate Northern Ireland parliament. They had wanted to defeat Home Rule completely, and keep the whole of Ireland an integral part of the United Kingdom. But they realised that they had little choice in the matter. In the House of Commons on 20 March 1920, Captain C. C. Craig (brother of the Unionist leader Sir James Craig, who would become the first Prime Minister of Northern Ireland) explained why they were reluctantly prepared to accept Partition:

'We believe that so long as we were without a Parliament of our own, constant attacks would be made upon us, and constant attempts would be made to draw us into a Dublin Parliament, and that is the last thing in the world that we desire to happen. We profoundly distrust the Labour Party and we profoundly distrust the Rt. Hon. Gentleman the Member for Paisley (Mr Asquith). We believe that if either of those parties, or the two in combination, were once more in power our chances of remaining a part of the United Kingdom would be very small indeed. We see our safety, therefore, in having a Parliament of our own, for we believe that once a Parliament is set up and working well, as I have no doubt it would in Ulster, we should fear no one.'

And so, in 1920, Parliament passed the Government of Ireland Act, which provided for the setting up of two governments and two parliaments in Ireland: in effect, partition. There would be one Irish Parliament at Stormont in Belfast to govern the six north-eastern counties of Antrim, Armagh, Down, Fermanagh, Londonderry and Tyrone, which were to form Northern Ireland as we know it today, and another in Dublin to govern the other twenty-six counties—today's Republic of Ireland. On 22 June 1921 the new Stormont Parliament was given a state opening by King George V, after an election that resulted in the return of forty Unionists and twelve Nationalists.

The early months of the new Northern Ireland state were marked by outbursts of sectarian violence in Belfast and elsewhere, for the Sinn Féin party refused to countenance Partition. In the South, the war was finally brought to an end by the Anglo-Irish treaty of December 1921. Under its provisions, an Irish Free State with Dominion status was set up, covering the whole of Ireland, but Northern Ireland was given the choice of opting out, which it exercised at once.

It is ironic now to reflect that the North, which had never wanted Home Rule, should have ended by getting it, while the South over the arrangement. The President of the Dáil, de ting independence instead.

The settlements did not bring an end to conflict. Apart from the severe rioting in Belfast, there was bitter dispute in the South over the arrangement. The President of the Dail, de Valera, refused to countenance a treaty which involved an oath of allegiance to the King, and went into opposition as the leader of a group of Republican hard-liners. Civil war broke out between the new government and the opposition in a resurgence of 'the Troubles'. There were many dark months of killings and counter-killings before the long Irish tradition of parliamentarianism reasserted itself.

The year 1921 is where I bring this brief review of Irish history to a close. Not that history stopped there—history does not stop anywhere. But it was where the ancient tensions between North and South, Anglo-Saxon and Celt, Protestant and Catholic, were frozen in constitutional amber.

How these tensions thaw out eventually will, I happen to believe, depend to an extent on the way in which the Irish— and the British—learn to look at Irish history. Politicians, for instance, all tend to use history for their own ends, to justify what they are doing in the present or what they would like to see done. For instance, Sinn Fein used the Easter Rising most astutely to hallow their separatist policies—despite the fact that the overwhelming majority of Irishmen at the time did not care about separation from Britain. The Sinn Feiners justified 1916 by appeals to the dead and to generations yet unborn—and with a constituency like that, they could hardly fail! At the same time, as Dr Conor Cruise O'Brien has argued (perhaps to his political cost), by making the Easter Proclamation the gospel of the Republic, Patrick Pearse's quasi-mystical concept of the need for violence and blood-sacrifice in every generation has become a justification not just for armed rebellions in the past but for violence and guerrilla warfare in the North today. In Ireland, as someone has said, history is a pack of tricks which the dead play on the living. Ireland is a land of epigrams as well as epitaphs.

In the Historiographical Revolution, Irish historians are slowly defusing Irish history on both sides of the Border as sacred writ to be cited as a categorical imperative to act in a certain way. We can only hope that eventually we will all learn to place the right emphasis on history as history, on mythology as mythology—and on today as today.

Books for Further Reading

This list does not purport to be a comprehensive bibliography of Irish history; rather, it is a note of some of the publications that I myself found most illuminating, and which I think other readers would find helpful if they wish to pursue the subject further.

Buckland, P: *Irish Unionism* (Gill and Macmillan, 1973)

Carty, James, (ed.): *Ireland from the Flight of the Earls to Grattan's Parliament* (C. J. Fallon, 1949)

Edwards, R. Dudley: *Daniel O'Connell and his World* (Thames and Hudson, 1975)

Edwards, R. Dudley: *Patrick Pearse* (Gollancz, 1977)

Hawthorne, James: *Two Centuries of Irish History* (BBC Publications, 1966)

Longford, F. P. and O'Neill, T.: *Eamonn de Valera* (Hutchinson, 1926)

Lyons, F. S. L.: *The Fall of Parnell* (Routledge and Kegan Paul, 1960)

Lyons, F. S. L.: *Ireland since the Famine* (Fontana, 1973)

Mansergh, Nicholas: *The Irish Question, 1840–1921* (Allen and Unwin, 1969)

Maxwell, Constantia: *Irish History from Contemporary Sources* (Allen and Unwin, 1923)

Maxwell, Constantia: *The Stranger in Ireland* (Jonathan Cape, 1954)

Moody, T. W. and Martin, F. X. (ed.): *The Course of Irish History* (The Mercier Press, 1967)

O'Brien, Conor Cruise (ed.): *The Shaping of Modern Ireland* (Routledge and Kegan Paul, 1960)

O'Brien, R. Barr: *Life of C. S. Parnell* (Smith, Elder and Co, 1898)

Woodham-Smith, Cecil: *The Great Hunger* (Hamish Hamilton, 1962)

In addition I warmly recommend the admirable series of *Educational Facsimiles* published by the Public Record Office of Northern Ireland.

Acknowledgements

Thanks are due for permission to quote extracts from the following copyright material: G. K. Chesterton, *Ballad of the White Horse*, page 79; John Devoy, *Devoy's Post Bag, 1871–1928*, Vol. I (C. J. Fallon, 1948), pages 99 and 100; W. B. Yeats, 'Come Gather Round Me Parnellites', page 109 and 'Easter 1916', page 134; the extract from a letter by G. B. Shaw on page 130 is printed with permission of the Society of Authors as agent for the Bernard Shaw Estate; the extract from a letter by Mabel McConnell on page 129 is taken from *The Memoirs of Desmond FitzGerald 1913–1916* (Routledge & Kegan Paul, 1968), edited by F. FitzGerald.

Many of the extracts quoted in Part I are taken from non-copyright material reproduced in Constantia Maxwell's *Irish History from Contemporary Sources* (George Allen & Unwin, 1923).

Thanks are due to the following for permission to reproduce black-and-white photographic material: National Library of Ireland for the Dutch watercolour painting of Irish men and women, Oliver Cromwell's letter to Colonel David Sinott, an Irish peasant cabin in the 1770s, Daniel O'Connell, and a cartoon from *The Pilot*, 1885; Viscount Massereene and Ferrard for 'King Billy' (William III) (D.207/16/26); Franciscan Friary, Dan Mhuire, Killiney for Patrick Sarsfield, Earl of Lucan; British Library for the first page of the Treaty of Limerick; D. A. C. Smith, Esq. for the Irish House of Commons 1790–1800 (EF47); Public Record Office of Northern Ireland for Theobald Wolfe Tone, and the British Prime Minister threatening the Chancellor of the Irish Exchequer; Her Majesty's Stationery Office for Lord Castlereagh's list of 31 boroughs, Unionist propaganda poster denouncing the Land League (D.2733), and Unionist crowds at the Ulster Convention, Balmoral, Belfast (CAB11/2); *Illustrated London News* for the impression of a post-Famine eviction scene, the great emigration to America, Waterloo Docks, Liverpool, Gladstone introducing the first Home Rule Bill, 1886, and the Ulster Volunteer Force in possession of Larne Harbour; the late Hon. Denis Craig MBE for the Ulster Unionist propaganda postcard *c.* 1912 (D.1415/E/21); National Museum of Ireland for Patrick Henry Pearse by Sean O'Sullivan, RHA; Radio Times Hulton Picture Library for British soldiers in a Dublin street during the 1916 Easter uprising, Sackville Street after being shelled by a British gunboat, and Dáil Eireann 1919.

The maps on pages 34, 39 and 47 are based, with additions and deletions, on maps appearing in *The Course of Irish History* by T. W. Moody and F. X. Martin (The Mercier Press, 1967) and the map on page 29 is based, with deletions, on the one appearing in *The Making of Modern Ireland* by J. C. Beckett (Faber and Faber, 1966).

INDEX